I Hate The Zoo

I Hate The Zoo

BO CHANCEY

PRESS

I Hate the Zoo
Published by 41Press

© 2017 by Bo Chancey

1 3 5 7 9 10 8 6 4 2

For information or bulk sales contact:

Manchester Christian Church
56 Old Bedford Road
Bedford, NH 03110

603-641-0124

bochancey@manchesterchristian.com

ISBN: 978-0-9968757-3-8

CONTENTS

WARNING

Everyone told me not to do it.

They said, "Don't go there. It won't work. You'll ruin your career."

I honestly had never even heard of Manchester, NH. I am a Texas boy. Born and bred in Texas. Educated in Texas. I had never lived anywhere but Texas, and my entire family was in Texas.

I wasn't looking to move. I had a fantastic job with an amazing church. I did not even have a resume, and I had never interviewed with another church. Then, out of the blue, my boss called me into his office and told me about this church in Manchester, NH.

Something leapt in my spirit though the very first time I heard about Manchester Christian Church. I called my wife and said, "I think we are moving to Manchester." She asked, "Where is that?" I said, "It is in New Hampshire." She asked, "Where is that?" I said, "I think that it is north of Boston." She said, "There's something north of Boston?"

My wife and I had never visited New England, but we had heard stories. People said that New England was a pastor's graveyard. They said that building a church in New England was like plowing concrete. They said that New England was post-Christian.

I was not sure what post-Christian meant, so I started asking around. It turns out that nobody really knows what it means. It is just kind of a phrase Christians use to describe a region where people do not attend church.

It is true. People in New Hampshire do not go to church. New Hampshire is the most irreligious state in the country. Less than 25% of New Hampshire's one million residents describe themselves as being religious, and only about 4% identify as evangelical Christians. Studies indicate that New Hampshire is the least generous state in the United States in regards to charitable contributions but in the top six in per capita income. While the rest of the country is spending time and money at church, New Hampshirites are riding their snowmobiles to their lake houses for the weekend.

Events unfolded quickly. Within a couple of months of first hearing about the church, the leaders of the church as well as my family discerned that I was being called by God to be their new senior pastor. My predecessor had been there for thirty years, and the church has grown to over 1,000 people. It was the biggest church in New Hampshire, but the leadership was preparing for the potential exodus that can come with a senior pastor change. It is not unusual for a church to drop 30% in the first couple of years of a new regime.

Sitting in the church before my first sermon there, I was struck by the realization that those people had no idea who I was. At 37, I was almost 30 years younger than my predecessor, and coming from Texas, I was definitely an outsider. I had a sermon on my heart to preach, but I realized that I had not planned what my first words to the church would be.

First words are important. I know better than to begin a message with "Good morning" or any other lame, canned statement. Jesus started the Sermon on the Mount with "Blessed are the poor in spirit." He came out firing with something that was on everyone's mind. He grabbed their attention and hearts by saying, "Let me tell you how to be happy even when you are poor."

Jesus did not mail in His introduction. He did not stand up, clear His throat, adjust His tunic and say: "Good morning. Welcome to the Mount. My name is Jesus. I am the Son of God. It is a glorious day here beside the Sea of Galilee, and in just a moment I am going to speak on being happy. Before I do though, we have just a couple of announcements. Peter? Where's Peter? There he is. Everybody give Peter a round of applause. His wife just had a baby. Way to go Peter! Also, I just received this note from our ushers. If you parked at dock B slip 41…you left your sail up."

First words matter, and I had not planned any. I walked on stage after being introduced, and the reception was less than stellar. Most arms were folded across their chests as they glared at the new kid. I prayed for wisdom and then said the only thing I could think of.

I simply said, "I love Jesus."

They responded with a standing ovation.

That was when I realized that people were wrong about New Hampshire. New Hampshire is not post-Christian. It is post-religious. People are desperate for Jesus but done with religion. They are hungry for the simple truths of having a relationship with God but unimpressed by religious intellectualism and ceremony.

That day, I invited the church to join me in praying for One. Praying for One is simply asking God every day to give you One person to share His love with. I told them that if we prayed that way that God would double our church.

And He did. In fact, He did more. We've tripled in size and have baptized over 2,500 people in six years.

Some people are utterly amazed that we are having such success in a post-religious context, but I would argue that it is actually easier to build God's kingdom in a place where religion is dead. There are no "cultural Christians" in New Hampshire. If you love Jesus here…you really love Him and are committed to doing His will. People are not playing religious games but are desperate to share God's love with their family, friends, neighbors and coworkers.

I am glad that the rest of the country is headed where New England already is because I know what God can do when religion is out of the equation.

What about your heart? Is religion out of the equation for you? God wants you to be post-religious so that you enjoy a relationship with Him.

I'll warn you ahead of time that this book should offend any religious sensibilities you are holding onto. I implore you not to let that freak you out. It is okay to think, wrestle, disagree and maybe even throw the book across the room. (However I do not recommend doing that if you are using an e-reader. I cannot be held responsible for broken screens.)

So take a deep breath and pray, "God, show me what you can do when religion is dead."

DEATH

Do not grieve over religion. Do not waste a single tear.
Religion served its purpose. Now it is time to disappear.

Those who fight for religion are the ones who profit most.
They are holding onto a corpse...trying to animate a
ghost.

Stop toying with religion. Enjoy a better Way instead. Be
free to embrace the living by releasing what is dead.

Religion stinks, because it's rotten...a decaying mass of
death. There was never life in religion, because it never
had a breath.

Do not fret over religion. There is no need to fear.
Religion served its purpose. Now it is time to disappear.
– Shiloh Battles

PUT THE BUNNY DOWN

It was the time between Halloween and Thanksgiving, when there is crispness in the night air announcing the impending change of seasons. I was at a magical age…old enough to ride a bike without training wheels but not old enough to ride it in the street.

Dad was a high school football coach, and it was his favorite time of year. He was busy getting the team ready and focused on making the best of what was left of the season.

Mom was a teacher, and with both parents working, it meant that my older sister and I had to have a babysitter each day after school. It was only for a couple of hours a day, but at that age, life can change dramatically in just a couple of hours.

We called our babysitters Ma and Pa. They were a retired couple that raised rabbits on their property. They had a large backyard lined with rabbit cages along the back edge with a forest beyond. My sister and I mostly played outside, and Ma and Pa simply asked that we remain in the yard and out of the woods.

Well, like all red-blooded American kids, we had rebellious streaks just long enough to break a few rules without causing any lasting damage, so when we went outside we headed straight for the woods.

My sister was much faster than me. She was older, taller and much leaner. At that age, I was not much of a runner. I suppose if I was running downhill with gravity's assistance I might have kept up with her, but on a flat surface she was way ahead. She rushed off into the woods as I yelled for her to wait up.

I remember pausing at the rabbit cages for a little visit. It looked like a bunny prison, and I liked to imagine what they were in for. "Ah, look at you...you got busted for stealing carrots from Mr. McGreggor's garden, didn't you?" I did not wait for a response but dashed off into the woods instead.

I found my sister a few yards in, crouched down with her back toward me. She was very still, and it looked like she was holding something. As I approached, calling her name, she looked over her shoulder and shushed me.

I asked what she was doing, and she said, "Nothing." I asked what she had in her hands, and she said, "Nothing." But I knew that "nothing" meant "something."

I pleaded with her to let me see, and when she finally turned around and opened her hands my breath was taken away.

All I could say was, "Ahh...bunny."

She had the tiniest, cutest, little baby bunny resting in her hands. I just wanted to grab it and hold it and love it and make it mine. My sister and I agreed that this bunny had to come home with us. After all, we found him fair and square alone in the woods. He needed us, and we needed him.

But there were problems. First off, we had to explain to Ma and Pa where we found the bunny. We were not allowed in the woods, so we needed to pretend that we found the bunny in the yard. This proved to be a crucial detail since we found out later that Ma and Pa threw the runts of the litter into the woods to die. Since they thought this bunny had made it back into the yard, they thought he might be strong enough to survive and agreed to let us ask our Mom if we could keep him. That brought the second problem.

Mom.

How in the world could we possibly convince Mom? There was not much time before her arrival, so we needed to put together a game plan fast. Our approach was neither creative nor elegant, but it was effective.

When Mom arrived, I rushed out of the house first to greet her. I met her at the car with a warm, "Good afternoon, Mother. How was your day?"

Mom, of course, knew something was up and asked, "What do you want?"

I said, "Oh nothing, Mother. I am just so glad to see you, and I was wondering if you had any chores I could help with when we get home."

It was overkill, but I was desperate and still young enough to not understand the importance of subtlety. That's when my sister stepped into action. What she did was bold, simple and sheer genius. She had the bunny behind her back and blurted out, "Mom, we found a bunny and Ma and Pa said we could keep it if it was okay with you."

Mom took a breath before saying "no" and during that breath my sister saved the day. She took the bunny from behind her back and held it up for my mother to see. Mom took one look at the bunny and said, "Ahh…bunny!"

We had her. There was no way she could say no. Mom said that we could take it home and then check with Dad to see if he approved. I think Mom was counting on Dad being the bad guy.

On the way home, my sister and I decided to name our bunny Friday since we found him on a Friday. It was not the most clever name, but honestly we never expected to make it far enough to name him. Dad had a football game that night and would not be home until late. We would have to wait until Saturday to see if Friday could be a permanent member of the family.

When we arrived home, my sister and I played with Friday until Mom said it was time for bed. We began to argue about who would get to sleep with Friday when Mom said that Friday would be sleeping in the garage. We decided not to press our luck and simply said, "Yes, Ma'am." We prepared a shoebox for Friday to sleep in and put him on top of the washing machine in the garage for the night. We kissed him good night and went off to bed.

I slept like a champ that night. Nothing produces better sleep than sweet bunny dreams. I woke up early the next morning and went to get my sister so that we could play with Friday. We rushed out to the garage and opened the shoebox. There Friday was… sleeping peacefully…so still…so cute. We said, "Wake up, Friday. It's time to play."

He didn't move.

We gently shook him.

He still didn't move.

We picked him up.

He was cold and stiff.

Something was wrong. My sister decided that Friday must be frozen. This seemed reasonable to me since the garage was pretty cold. We decided to give Friday a hot bath to unfreeze him, so we went into the bathroom and ran some hot water. The bath loosened him up a bit, but he still wasn't waking up. We decided to use the blow dryer to dry him off.

Mom and Dad were sound asleep down the hall, but the sound of the hair dryer must have woken Mom up. She came blurry-eyed into the bathroom to find out what was going on, and it took a couple of moments for the situation to fully register. We explained that Friday was frozen, and we were trying to warm him up.

Mom said, "That rabbit's not frozen…he's dead!"

That is when Mom jumped into action. She had me run out to the garage to get the shoebox that had been Friday's bed. It would now serve as his coffin, and my sister went to get the shovel. We were quiet since it was still early and Dad was sleeping. We went outside and around to the side of our house where we dug a shallow grave and had a simple funeral for our bunny Friday who died on Saturday.

Then I went inside and had a bowl of Fruit Loops and watched cartoons. The rest of the day was a typical Saturday. We ran some errands and did some chores. I watched football on TV with my Dad and went to bed. Friday did not cross any of our minds, and nobody bothered mentioning him to Dad.

The next morning we got up and went to church. After church we went home for lunch, and I put my play clothes on to go outside. I was not outside for very long before I got bored. There was nobody to play with. My friends were not around, and my sister wasn't interested.

That's when I remembered Friday. I knew exactly where he was. I grabbed the shovel and went around to the side of the house. It only took a moment to dig up Friday, then I had him in my hands once again.

Friday wasn't as much fun to play with as before, so I had to get creative. I decided to play catch. I threw Friday as high as I could, then tried to catch him. I missed a few times, and Friday was starting to look pretty ragged.

That's when my dad came outside looking for me. He called my name from the front of the house, but I did not respond. He called again, and I did not respond. He called a third time, and I yelled back that I was busy.

I think this confused my dad. What could his son possibly be busy with? Besides that, I was supposed to come when Dad called. This was nonnegotiable.

Dad came around the house to find out what was going on. He looked at me and asked what I was doing. I explained that I was playing with Friday. He asked, "Who is Friday?" And I showed him.

This time there was no, "Ahh…bunny!" There was only shocked and confused silence as my father looked at me with a concerned expression that is difficult to put into words.

He finally spoke and said, "Put the bunny down."

I didn't want to put the bunny down. I was playing with the bunny. The bunny was my friend.

My dad took a step toward me, and I held Friday closer. Dad froze and calmly said, "Put the bunny down, son."

He repeated himself and edged closer to me. I finally set Friday down on the ground, and my dad scooped me up in his arms and rushed me into the house to wash up. While Mom gave me a bath, Dad buried the bunny deep into the ground, then he came in to have a chat.

He gave some important life wisdom that day when he simply said, "Son…we don't play with dead things."

It is true. We don't play with dead things. Dead things are gross, decaying and are not meant to be played with.

Dads do not want their children to play with dead things. God the Father does not want His children to play with dead things.

Religion is one of those things.

Religion is dead, and God does not want us playing with it anymore. When we let go of religion we are free to fall into the Father's arms by embracing a relationship with Jesus. We were created to be in a relationship with God, and this relationship brings life to our decaying world.

Our world is out of sync with its Creator. A simple look at the evening news reveals that things are not right with this world.

I hate watching the news. Every time I watch the news, I end up depressed for several days. It seems like all we have in this world is BAD news. You know the standard evening news format: terrorism, domestic violence, economic turmoil, political unrest and at the top of the hour…family pets being held for ransom. Follow that up with a water-skiing squirrel for a little levity, and you have the NEWS.

If the evening news even vaguely represents a "day-in-the-life" of the world we live in, it would be impossible to deny that things are not as they should be. This world is messed up. It is out of order. It cannot possibly be as the Creator intended. The problem is that we keep playing with dead things.

Do you ever find yourself looking around and saying, "This just isn't right"? A world that is filled with pain, hunger, disease, greed and all kinds of human atrocities just can't be right. Something has gone horribly wrong.

Religion is a human attempt to deal with what is wrong in our world. We create religious systems to help us make sense of what is happening. We use religion to provide made up answers and to guilt people into submission.

Religion is not the answer. In fact, religion is often a catalyst for our problems. People do heinous things to one another in the name of religion. Religion can be just another system of abuse. People use religion to manipulate and take advantage of others in attempts to gain power and control. Instead of eradicating sin, religion tends to exacerbate sin.

I often hear people talking about going back to "the good old days." They desire to see culture return to some previous state of being, but they generally do not understand that they are romanticizing an earlier time. They believe that if we were more religious things would be better, but things were not better. They were bad, and religion did not help. That is why people abandoned religion and are looking for a better answer.

What was meant to be a beautiful, fluid and perfect display of God's power and creativity has been thrown completely out of whack by the rebellion of humankind. God is not one to sit back and allow the madness to continue without taking drastic action. It is still God's intent for this world to return to the perfect rhythm and balance He created it for. This all begins with you and me. That's right; it starts with us. In order for all creation to be restored to its proper order, we must return to an eternal relationship with God.

Relationship is greater than religion. Religion makes no provision for the removal of sin, but a relationship with Jesus deals with sin and death once and for all.

Sin is a universal problem. The devastating effects of sin touch all people throughout time. Romans 3:23 tells us that "All have sinned and fallen short of the glory of God." Every person who has ever lived has sinned except for one solitary exception. There is only one who was sinless, and His name is Jesus. Hebrews 4:15 puts it this way, "For we do not have a high priest who is unable to sympathize with our weaknesses, but we have one who has been tempted in every way, just as we are—yet was without sin."

But maybe you are kind of wondering, "What is sin exactly?" Sin is anything you do that God forbids or anything you do not do that God commands. Sin is not a difficult thing to figure out. In fact Galatians 5:19 says, "The acts of the sinful nature are OBVIOUS…" (Emphasis mine). Sin is no mystery.

We all know what sin is, and most of us are very adept at sinning. I know that I have been a bit of a "sin practitioner" in my life, and my guess is that you too know the pleasures of a good, old-fashioned sin. We sin because we like it. When we sin, we are making a choice to break our relationship with God. We are choosing the temporary pleasures of sin over the eternal oneness found in an unblemished relationship with the Creator of the world. It seems like an unbelievably silly choice, yet all of us make it, and the consequences are devastating.

Sin ushered DEATH into this world and death touches us all. Romans 5:12 says, "Therefore, just as sin entered the world through one man, and death through sin, and in this way death came to all men, because all sinned." The imperfection of sin separates us from the perfection of God. All the longing, straining and human effort will never bring that perfection back. The devastating consequence of sin has left us powerless. There is nothing we can do on our own to restore the broken relationship with God and escape the death that results from sin.

Just in case you haven't noticed yet…this is a PROBLEM! Sin is a problem for us and a problem for God. God created us to be in relationship with Him, and when that relationship is broken, He desperately longs to restore it. In the same way, our hearts long for reunion with God. Without Him we are incomplete and empty.

Nothing completes us, and our efforts toward happiness and self-fulfillment always fall short leaving us with an incessant desire for more. This is a problem that we are utterly powerless to solve, but God steps in and makes a Way back to Him.

God makes the way for salvation. It cannot be earned or achieved. It can only be received.

Think of it this way. Is there anything you can do to remove sin from your life? Is there any kind of religious activity that would make a difference? What if you never sinned again? What if from this day forward you never again disobeyed God? Would sin be removed? Of course not, because you have already sinned. You cannot go back in time and stop yourself from sinning. It simply isn't possible.

Now maybe you are thinking, "Hey, now. Hold on a second, mister. I'm not that bad of a guy. Seriously, I know people who are way more sinful than me. It's not like I've killed anybody or done anything heinously wrong. Cut me some slack."

I have actually heard people say, "Come on...nobody is perfect. I know I've sinned, but it's not that bad. It's not like I am an axe murderer."

When "axe murderer" becomes your point of comparison, you know that you are in trouble. There is no value in comparative holiness. Being "better" than anyone else means nothing because perfection is the standard.

With God perfection is the key because He is PERFECT. Think about it. What would happen if God, who is perfect, united Himself with someone who is imperfect? Would perfection or imperfection win out? Imperfection always wins, and this is why:

The smallest imperfection makes the greatest perfection completely imperfect.

Consider a sheet of white paper that is free from any marks or defects. One could argue that it is perfectly white. What would happen if you put one black dot somewhere on that paper? Would the paper still be perfectly white? No? But come on, it is almost all white. It is 99.9999999% white, but is it perfect? Nope! The smallest perfection makes the greatest perfection completely imperfect.

The same is true with God. He is the greatest perfection and our imperfection makes it impossible for us to be with Him. This grieves God because He created you to be in relationship with Him. You belong with God. This is a problem that only God can fix.

His solution is Jesus. God became like us to make a way for us to become like Him.

Jesus was born of a virgin. He lived a sinless life. He loved deeply, taught powerfully and compassionately performed mighty miracles. Jesus was perfect. He was fully human and yet fully God. Jesus felt pain, faced temptation and experienced everything found in the human condition. Jesus allowed Himself to be arrested, falsely accused, mocked, beaten and crucified. Jesus even died. Death is the consequence of sin. Death is separation from perfection. What happened on that cross is the single most important event in all of human history. Jesus became sin.

The One who was perfect took my sin, your sin and the sin of all humankind upon Himself, and He died. Jesus became imperfect, was separated from the Father and took the consequence we deserve. Jesus died, and sin died. They buried Jesus, but the best was still to come.

Jesus did not stay dead. No, the Creator...the life-giver... the One who spoke everything into existence...The Word... conquered death! Jesus rose from the dead because He is LIFE! He rose victoriously because He rose perfect. Imperfection (sin) died on that cross and stayed dead, but Jesus came back to life. Scripture tells us that He returned to His Father and sent His Holy Spirit to dwell inside all who belong to Him.

This is God's solution to our death problem. He did what we were powerless to do. Jesus defeated sin so that we could be made perfect. Perfection is still the standard, and it is not something that you can attain on your own. It only comes through Jesus. When we surrender our lives to Jesus and unite ourselves to Him, the Holy Spirit fills us and we are made completely perfect! When God looks at us, He sees Himself, and He is perfect. We are then free to approach God and live in relationship with Him, just as He intended from the beginning.

Maybe at this point, you are starting to wonder, "Okay, so what do I do? Where do I start?"

Receiving grace, forgiveness and salvation begins with one of the greatest words ever...repent. Repentance is way more than feeling bad or sorry for sinning. It is more than making a commitment to try not to sin anymore. Repentance entails a completely fresh and new start. It is a choice to have your entire world view changed. Romans 12:2 tells us to "[b]e transformed by the renewing of your mind". Repentance means that we get to live for God instead of anything else. Repentance means that the number one most important thing in our lives is our relationship with God. Repentance means that we are restored to the place God intended for us to be from the beginning.

If you want to see change in this world, it all begins with your choice today. Be restored, be made new and find perfection through Jesus. Life will make sense only when you make peace with the God of the Universe. God loves you, and no matter who you are or what you've done or what's been done to you…God has a place for you in His family.

Pray right now. Confess to God that you have sinned. Tell Him how much you want to have a relationship with Him. Acknowledge that on your own you are powerless over sin. Repent from sin and your former way of thinking. Ask God to change the way you think and your entire world view. Ask God to make you perfect through His Holy Spirit living in you. Ask God to restore you into a right relationship with Him.

Put the bunny down. Put down the death of sin and religion so that you are free to hold onto life through a relationship with Jesus.

SINNER OR SAINT?

I hate the zoo.

I know that you are probably thinking, "Who could possibly hate the zoo?"

Well, I do. That's who. I hate the zoo!

I remember my first zoo trip. I could not wait to get there. I had visions of magnificent beasts doing magnificently beastly things. I pictured alligators prowling the waters, tigers pouncing on their prey and lions roaring mightily. I was so excited that I could not sleep the night before.

When I arrived at the zoo, I quickly found a map and ran to the center of the zoo where the lions lived. There was a high fence and a deep ditch separating me from the lion's habitat. I thought to myself, "That's right. They need to protect me. I would be a tasty treat for a hungry lion."

I peered into the lion's home with deep anticipation, but I did not see any lions. I then noticed that there was a dark cave located atop a hill. I thought: "Yes, that's right. The lions are in the cave." So I waited.

Two hours later, one lion finally emerged from the cave. I was ecstatic. I would finally hear the majestic roar of the king of the jungle. The lion came forth, and his mane shimmered in the noonday sun. As he stretched himself and lifted his head, I prepared myself for the deafening roar that would soon follow.

But do you know what that lion did? He yawned. Then he laid down on a rock and went back to sleep. I was furious! How could he? How dare he? He was supposed to roar, and instead he yawned like an overgrown house cat.

I screamed, "You're no lion," and I left to find the alligators.

When I got to the alligators I was pleased to discover several of them out in the water. I could see their beady eyes peering just above the surface. Finally I would see some action, so I waited.

One hour later not one single alligator had moved. Birds landed on their faces, and they did not budge. Several kids threw pennies at their eyes, and they never even blinked. I noticed on the backs of several of them, there was old chewing gum that looked like it had been there for weeks. I became convinced that the zoo had replaced real alligators with fakes. Nothing could be completely still for that long.

When it was time to go, I had seen nothing more than a handful of animals napping in the shade. There was no activity. There was no life. The zoo appeared dead. I was devastated, and that is why I hate the zoo.

Animals do not act like animals are supposed to act at the zoo.

That is problem with religion. Religion seeks to tame and enslave. Religion looks like death, and that is why more and more people want nothing to do with it. They check it out but do not find the answers and life they expected. They become frustrated and want nothing to do with religion.

We are living in a progressively post-religious cultural context. Religion is losing its place in society, and the void is causing some to panic. Some religious leaders equate post-religious with post-Christian, but loving Jesus is on the rise not the decline. Rejecting religion is not the same as rejecting God.

The doom and gloom prognosticators are declaring an end to Christianity. That fear mongering nonsense needs to stop. Christianity is not dead. It is incapable of dying because it is based on Christ's resurrection and His promise of eternal life. God made a promise, and God cannot lie. These two realities serve as anchors for our souls. Remember them so that you are not set adrift on the sea of doubt.

Religion, on the other hand, is most assuredly dead. Don't panic. It is for the best. If you love Jesus, then the death of religion is a fantastic reality to live in. The gospel of Jesus will thrive in a post-religious context. Institutional hierarchies and religious-based profit centers will surely crumble, but the gospel will more than survive. The Church is at its best under pressure and at its worst when it holds popular power.

Far too much energy is expended in attempts to preserve a preferred way of life. It is impossible to follow Jesus when our primary concern is to protect our perceived rights. Authentic Christ followers have laid down their rights and become slaves to Jesus. There should be no confusion on this particular point. Jesus said that if we desire to be His disciples we must lay down our lives, pick up our crosses and follow Him.

Never replace the wondrous joy of stumbling after Jesus with the pursuit of lifestyle advancement and maintenance. We know that we have fallen prey to this when our discussions begin to center around protecting our place and position instead of advancing the gospel. Local churches quickly become distracted with conversations about maintaining their tax-exempt statuses and navigating the newest legislation regarding morality. How many months, years and decades have been lost fighting the wrong fights?

Post-religious is not the same as post-Christian. Jesus did not come to establish a new religious system. He came to invite the world into a relationship with Him. Following Jesus is about becoming adopted sons and daughters who are eternal heirs to the kingdom of heaven. Access to God is not based on human merit. It is not about who we are and what we do. Access to God is about who Jesus is and what He did for us.

This whole grace thing blows religion out of the water. Grace is the only way that a relationship with God can exist. Grace is the only answer to the problem of sin.

Salvation is an all or nothing deal. We are either completely saved by grace through faith in Jesus or we are not saved at all. God initiates, maintains and completes our salvation. Salvation is based on who Jesus is, what Jesus did and what Jesus promised to do. We are recipients of grace who become participants in sharing grace.

Religion is what happens when we abandon grace. I am convinced that just about everyone is tempted to step away from grace at some point. Grace is good news. It is readily received and accepted. We begin to live in grace and experience the metamorphoses of our new identities in Christ, expressed from the inside out.

Then we forget.

We forget that God did the work. We become arrogant and indignantly proud. We look at our relatively clean lives and compare them to the filthy sinners around us. We think we look good. We think we have arrived at some pinnacle of personal purity. We spend our energy being disgusted with the sins of others while never noticing or grieving over own sin.

We abandon grace by becoming religious.

Jesus told a story about two sons and their father. The younger son asked his father for his inheritance so that he could leave home and do his own thing. The father gave the younger son the money and the son proceeded to squander the money on wild living. The son ran out of money and had nothing to eat. He finally came to his senses and decided to go home to see if his father would allow him to become a servant in his household. He was nervous about seeing his father because he had no right to come home. He had disgraced the family name and wasted half the family's wealth, but when he was still a long way off, his father spotted him and came running. The father restored his lost son to the family and threw a massive party to celebrate.

This story is often referred to as the parable of the Prodigal Son, but I think that it is woefully mistitled. It should be the parable of the Graceful Father. The father is the central character. It is his story. His son rebels and disgraces the family name, but the father waits and watches for the son's return. When the father sees the son, he runs to him! He receives the son, welcomes him home and restores him to the family. The father rejoices and decides to throw a party.

But…there is an older brother. The older brother did not leave. The older brother did not disgrace the family name. The older brother stayed and worked in his father's fields. When he hears that his wayward brother has come home, he does not share in his father's happiness. Instead, he complains that the father has never thrown him a party. What he fails to understand is that the party is not for the prodigal, but for the father. It is the father's party.

This is a story of grace that shocked Jesus' listeners. The image of a father running to his son was shocking. The father's rebuke of the older brother was shocking. Jesus knew that we would struggle to remain in grace.

Older brothers forget that they were once prodigal sons. Older brothers believe that they are entitled to God's blessings. Older brothers think that they deserve God's favor.

At some point, everyone becomes the older brother, and older brothers are wrong.

Death is all we earn. Death is all we deserve. Death is the result of every bit of living that is done apart from grace.

How do you know if you have stepped away from grace? If you feel cheated…if you think God owes you something…if you believe that you are better than others…if you deny people grace… if you follow rules instead of Jesus…if you cannot celebrate when the Father celebrates…if you no longer grieve over your own sin… if you think there should be prerequisites to faith…if you think people should change before they are accepted…then grace has left your building. You may look the part, but death is decaying your insides.

Remember that the first step of faith is merely a step toward home. When someone decides they want to come home to the Father, He runs to receive and restore. People of grace rejoice over everyone who chooses to come home. People of grace participate in the Father's party.

Heaven is the Father's party. Heaven is not merely a faraway hope. It can be a present-day reality. Jesus taught us to pray, "Your kingdom come, your will be done, on earth as it is in heaven." Participants in grace are to prayerfully usher in and welcome the kingdom of heaven.

Do not allow your relationship with Jesus to become religious. Religion sucks the life out of everything, but a relationship with God breathes life into everything. We replace relationship with religion any time that we have tried to earn anything from God. Religion is a merit-based system, but relationship is a grace-based system.

Relationships are alive…religion is dead.

Relationships have options…religion does not.

Religious systems are rigid. They place labels on people in attempts to control. The rules control who is in and who is out. The rules control behavior. The rules control thoughts. The rules are lord. That is idolatry.

Relationships are fluid. People are not labeled because who they are is being discovered as their identity is uncovered and developed. Relationships require freedom. There must be freedom to question, to wonder and to explore. Relationships invite people to become something greater than they could ever be on their own. Relationships restore our souls.

Religion has no power to change you. It simply reveals what you already are. Religion is an external system that provides a point of reference for comparison. The value of religion is that it points to the beauty and power of relationship.

Rules and regulations serve as a mirror to reveal our flaws, but they cannot fix our flaws. Those who succeed in religious systems are the ones who do the best job of keeping the exterior squeaky clean. They maintain the outward appearance but never lift the hood to inspect the inner workings.

Religion is like slapping a fresh coat of paint on a classic car and calling it "restored." It might look shiny and new, but if it does not run properly it is not restored.

Jesus was pretty harsh with religious leaders. He referred them as "whitewashed tombs." His harshness was not mean-spirited but was necessary for them to understand the gravity of their situation. The Pharisees had done a good job of navigating the religious system they were working within. They worked hard to keep the exterior clean, but their insides were rotten.

Everyone's insides are rotten. We all need restoration from the frame up. When restoring a car, you must take it apart all the way to the frame. Every piece of the car is checked and then repaired or replaced in order to make the car new again.

Religion can reveal what is broken, but it cannot fix it. Religion merely reveals that you are a sinner and provides a system for you to compare yourself to others. If your relative sinfulness is at what you deem to be an acceptable level, then you attempt to maintain. It is a terrible burden though, because without restoration we are all in a steady state of decay. Our imperfections are revealed as we break down more and more.

Religion says you are worthless, but Jesus declares that you are restorable.

There is a well-intended religious sentiment that drives me absolutely bonkers. It goes something like this: "I am just a sinner saved by grace." There is just enough truth in the statement to make it easily accepted and eagerly repeated, but there is a deceptive twist of the truth that generally goes unnoticed and becomes a rotting root for destructive false teaching.

The issue is one of core identity. Who are you? Are you a sinner or a saint?

"I am just a sinner saved by grace" declares that your core identity is junk, but if you are truly saved by grace that cannot be accurate. The salvation Jesus provides transforms the core identity. Saved people are no longer sinners. The old is gone and the new has come. We are SAINTS!

Religion denies this new reality by attempting to hold you to your former identity. If you think that this is merely an issue of semantics and not a valid discussion, I assure you that you are wrong. This matters because identity is the foundation from which we live. If we have a flawed view of self, then we are doomed from inception. We cannot live the holy lives God redeemed us for. We cannot participate in the amazing works that He has prepared in advance for us to do. We remain in a state of junky-ness convinced that we are utterly worthless.

If I am JUST a sinner, then I have no choice but to sin. Sinners sin…it is what they do. Religion is great at pointing out sin, but it denies choice. A relationship with Jesus provides freedom to choose. Do I want to sin, or do I want to be a saint? Grace gives us freedom to choose. We can live by the old identity or the new identity.

If you have a relationship with Jesus, you cannot say, "I am just a sinner saved by grace." You can say, "I *was* a sinner saved by grace." Followers of Jesus cannot claim the sinner's identity any longer. To do so is to deny the very power of the cross of Christ. The issue of identity acceptance is paramount for following Jesus. We cannot live for Him if we refuse to accept the life He gives.

Religious people balk at the notion of sainthood. They want to believe that sainthood is reserved for only the religious elite who meet specific criteria based on human tradition. That is absolutely preposterous. Sainthood is rooted in the work of Jesus and is offered to all. It is not earned by an elite few.

Convincing people that they can never be more than junk is a religious power play designed to keep the masses in their place. "You dirty, rotten, filthy, worthless, no good sinners shouldn't even bother trying to follow Jesus because there is no hope for you. You should just depend on the leaders of your religious institution to mediate for you, tell you what to think and control you with fear." Religion is bondage, death and lies. Jesus is freedom, life and truth.

Jesus declares that you can be a saint. He takes junk and completely redeems it. He sees the restorative potential in everyone because He is the Creator of life. No matter where you've been or what you've done or what's been done to you…Jesus declares that His grace is sufficient for you. His plan is to restore you from the inside out.

He changes your core identity from sinner to saint. He takes you apart...right down to the frame and rebuilds. Everything is made new. This process is called sanctification. Justification is when we are saved by grace through faith. We are justified by the work of Jesus and are given new life through our relationship with Him. The relationship is secure because it is based on who Jesus is, what Jesus did and what Jesus promised to do. Living out the new identity of sainthood is the process of sanctification. Remnants of the old self are stripped away and replaced with holiness.

A relationship with Jesus allows us to declare, "I am a SAINT saved by grace." This is huge. Holding onto a sinner's identity denies you the opportunity to live for Jesus. If you are just a sinner then you will be content with sin. Sinners sin...it is what they do, but saints have options. It is not that saints never sin. We do not deny the reality of sin our lives, but we are not defined by that sin. We choose to accept the new reality of God's grace at work within us, and we have the opportunity to live abundant lives in Christ.

Religion convinces people that they are resigned to a sinful existence. Most people simply accept their personal sin as a reality they cannot escape, but Jesus told us to "be perfect therefore as your heavenly father is perfect." Why would Jesus tell us to do something that He would not make a way for us to do? On our own we are powerless over sin, but through our relationship with Jesus, His power is at work within us to overcome sin. We have a choice.

We do not have to sin today. Nowhere in the Bible does it say, "thou shalt sin every day." In fact, the scriptures are full of commands not to sin. Do not deny the power of Jesus and the new identity He provides. You do not have to sin today.

Think about it. Can you go one second without sinning? Can you go one minute without sinning? Can you go one hour without sinning? Of course you can. Set your mind on things above, not on earthly things. Take captive your thoughts and make them obedient to Jesus. Be aware of God's constant presence. Remember who you are…that you are a saint and not a sinner. Keep going one second, one minute, one hour at a time, and before you know it, a day without sin will come to pass.

You have a choice. Sinner or saint? One is death. The other is life. One is the foundation of religion and the other is the foundation of a relationship with God.

CONSUMERANITY

Church + Consumerism – Christ = Consumeranity

*Woe to those who peddle gods to make fat masses fatter.
They dole out hits of candy-coated religion...with no
substance to their matter.*

*Consumption prophets' profits soar with an enlarged
consumer base. Religion is not satisfied until it enslaves
the human race.*

*The only leading is off to slaughter on the altar of
consumption. Suckle the teat of selfishness...engorged
with fear and corruption.*

*Suckers suck. It's what they do. There's one born every
minute. Live by the teat. Die by the teat. Consuming has
no life in it.*

– Shiloh Battles

Church + Consumerism – Christ = Consumeranity

Consumerism is fantastic for driving a capitalist economy
but terrible for advancing the cause of Christ. The
primary identity of Jesus followers must be participants instead
of consumers. If we believe that we are primarily consumers of

God, then the commands of Jesus will not make much sense. We balk at any notion of sacrifice because it does not align with our core identities. Consumeranity reinforces the sinful nature while authentic Christianity puts the sinful nature to death.

The American Dream is a good example of this. The American Dream is essentially about personal advancement. We are taught that our primary purpose is to improve economically. Each generation should have a bigger house and more stuff than the previous generation so that we can "provide a better life for our children." It is an appealing notion that is easily digested and regurgitated.

I know people who are working themselves to death. They are slaving away in the name of "providing a better life" for their families. They have more stuff, but I am not so sure they are better off. Sometimes the realization of the American Dream is the realization that the dream can be a nightmare.

In the name of progress, we have created families where children never see their parents, where the pressure of consumer debt is crushing our souls and where busyness rules our days with unrelenting demands to feed the machine of consumerism.

This is not what we were created for. We were created by God to be in a relationship with God. He has life for us, but we often choose the death we already know over the unknown abundant life He promises.

This is where churches come into the equation. How churches respond to consumerism matters. If consumerism is embraced by the church and reinforced, then the core message of Christ is generally abandoned for things more easily consumed.

What happens when the church becomes more interested in promoting the American Dream than pursuing Jesus' mission? The church winds up broken. When you use something for a purpose that it is not designed for, you break it. Much of what we call "church" is broken.

Consumeranity is a fast-growing monstrosity. Just as consumerism propels and dictates every other facet of our lives, it often replaces Christ as the driving force in many churches. Meeting the consumerist needs of those already "saved" has become the number one purpose of numerous congregations.

The outlook is bleak if this alarming trend remains unchecked. At this very moment, Christ and His mission are being forced out of the church as more and more leaders bow to the temptation to cater to an ever-indulgent mass of churchgoers. If we continue to replace fulfilling Christ's mission with meeting the perceived needs of Christian consumers, we will end up with a church that is void of Christ. It will not resemble Jesus, and He will not be found within it. We will be left with Consumeranity.

Consumeranity is a nasty imitation of the real church. It masquerades in light and is highly appealing to the selfishly motivated. It makes sales pitches and promises that have nothing to do with dying to self but promotes the consumer- driven identity that is already present. Consumeranity targets its primary consumers and convinces them to find a church home that is "right for them." They have to find a church that will meet their needs and provide the best programming for their family. They need a church where they can feel comfortable and safe. The prevailing question eventually becomes: "Where can I get the most bang for my buck?"

Church leaders understand that this is what people are thinking, and in order to do the business of church well, they conform to the standards set before them. Churches begin to compete with one another over a dwindling consumer base, and all Hell breaks loose. Seriously…all Hell breaks loose. I am not attempting to be vulgar with my usage of the word "Hell." I mean it quite literally. When local churches view one another as competition, then we are experiencing Hell on earth because we have abandoned God's presence and mission for a nasty imitation. When the reality of Christ's church is not present in a culture, things go from bad to worse quickly.

When the focus becomes being "better" than the church down the block and the pressure builds to make this week's experience more spectacular than last week's, then the challenging truths of following Jesus begin to get replaced with fluffy notions that become the root of deep heresy and false doctrine. How else can you account for the prevalence of the "Health and Wealth" phenomenon? That consumerist nonsense has found its way into almost every corner of the mainline church. Even the most conservative churches often preach some version of the "give to get" message.

"If you tithe, God will bless you. If you serve, God will bless you. If you obey, God will bless you."

But the blessing does not get defined. Christian consumers are left to interpret what they believe that blessing to be, and they usually end up thinking that it has to do with the accumulation of more stuff. That can be a pretty popular message for those who already know Christ. They like that concept and readily buy into it because it feeds their consumerist tendencies. Somewhere along the way we combined "The American Dream" with capitalist economics and a smattering of Jesus and came up with the Come-to-Jesus-and-all-your-wildest-dreams-will-come-true gospel.

It doesn't work though, and the Christian consumer is left wanting. They obey, but where is their blessing? They tithe, but an extra twenty grand doesn't magically appear in their bank accounts. They serve, but it isn't as fun as they were promised. So they leave to find a "better" church.

The evolvement of the "Church Shopper" is perhaps the clearest indictment that Consumeranity has ravaged our culture. Christian consumers bounce from church to church in hopes that all their wildest church dreams will one day come true. They never find true fellowship, authentic accountability or sustained biblical teaching. They will leave as soon as something they don't like happens.

If the pastor forgets to shake their hand, they leave. If the youth minister says the word "crap," they bolt. If the music is too loud, too fast, too soft or too slow, they head for the doors. If they get offended, have their toes stepped on or feel ignored, they are gone. If nobody calls them when they decide to leave, then they will come back for two more weeks just so they can leave again.

Church shoppers often tell me that they left their home church because they didn't really feel connected. They tell me that after they decided to leave the church nobody even noticed. I always share with them that I know how they can fix that problem if they are a part of our church. All they need to do is serve every week so that we are counting on them. Then we will notice when they are gone. Nobody I have shared that with has ever come back, but we didn't really notice.

I once met a family of die-hard church shoppers. Over a six-month period of time, they visited 25 churches but still couldn't find a church home. Somewhere along the way, they were taught that they needed to find "the perfect church." So this family bounced around from church to church week after week, searching for something they would never find. As I looked at that precious family, I became nauseated by the damage being done to them. Each church along the way made their little sales pitch and tried to convince them to stay, but they always found something they didn't like. I asked what they were looking for in a church, and everything they said reeked of Consumeranity. I strongly encouraged them to just pick a church, any church, and to throw their lives into the mission of Jesus Christ.

Now deep down, I wanted them to pick my church. We were number 26 on their list, so I figured they were getting desperate and that we might actually have a shot. FYI, we didn't win, but that is the craziest thing about Consumeranity…nobody wins. Churches scramble to compete for the affection of the church shopper and ultimately lose sight of their true mission. Church shoppers are left to wander aimlessly through a vast sea of Christian marketing and propaganda never to find the sweet joy of authentic connection within the Body of Christ.

Over the last several years, I have asked hundreds of guests what they were looking for in a church. Only once have I had someone tell me that they were seeking a church home where their gifts could be maximized to move Christ's kingdom forward. Every other person was looking for something they could consume. They wanted a specific program, a certain ministry, a style of music, a particular size, etc. It makes you start to wonder: Is Jesus really enough? It seems that in today's church market the presence of God takes a back seat to a myriad of more "pressing issues."

Consumeranity is flourishing. It is big business that feeds off of the selfishness of its loyal brethren. Churches are competing with one another for the eager Christian consumer. They are pushing out products that are designed to lure church shoppers into their buildings while neglecting Christ's mission to seek and save those who are lost. We have equated church success with church growth regardless of what it costs. It may cost us Christ, but who cares as long as we are the biggest, richest, hippest church on the block?

Jesus cares.

He wants His church to grow more than anyone, but if it is not rooted in Him, then it isn't really His church. Jesus is enough. His gospel is good news. His invitation to participate with Him in building His kingdom is gloriously wonderful news. People are desperate for the genuine article. We must refrain from selling cheap knock-offs.

If Jesus cares, we should care too.

Avoid the temptation to turn following Jesus into another dead religious activity. Consumeranity may be the hottest new religion on the market, but it is not the answer, and it will not last. Hold firmly to the beauty of a dynamic relationship with God and do not be deceived into thinking you are immune to the allure of Consumeranity.

The plague of Consumeranity has found its way into churches of all sizes and types. Immunity seems to have eluded us all. In desperate attempts to survive, small churches are forced to feed the Christian consumer. In order to stay on top and support their infrastructures, mega churches fall prey to keeping the customer happy. Everyone seems to be scrambling to find a niche in the marketplace.

Consumerism is always based on the quick and easy fix. We want immediate results that cost us very little, and under no circumstances are we willing to endure pain to achieve our desired results. Infomercials provide some of the best examples of this. My favorite is for the "Seven Minute Abs."

We are a culture of "seven minute abs" junkies. We love the notion of the quick fix and will gladly buy any shortcut to immediate success. We want what we want when we want it, and we don't want to work for any of it. "Give it to me now," we scream, "And while you are at it, make it easy." We are the life-over-easy generation, and because of that, we are overindulged, deceived and selfish.

I am amazed at how advertisers market products to us. Are we really dumb enough to believe that we can have amazing six-pack abs in seven minutes a day? There is not one product in the entire world that will make you look like the people on T.V. in just seven minutes a day. It is not possible. Thirty minutes a day won't do it either. We are not idiots. We know that the only way to achieve a sculpted body is through a total lifestyle change. You have to eat healthy foods in moderation and work out for hours each day. It is not easy, and it doesn't come cheap. Real results cost. They require sacrifice, dedication and time. These are all things that we are reluctant to give up. We know all of that, but for some delusional reason, we hold onto the false hope that the quick fix will work.

We invest in worthless junk only to be continually disappointed by failure. You know the mantras of our easy way out society: "Get the car you deserve today," "Consolidate your debt for pennies on the dollar," "Meet your mate with one easy click of the mouse," "Look the way you have always dreamed without breaking a sweat." They market this garbage to us because we buy it. The truth always seems too simple. We don't like simple. We want the formula or magic potion for success.

Take your finances for example. In order to be financially successful, there is really only one governing principle. Spend less than you earn. That's it. It is not complicated. It requires a disciplined commitment to the principle. It works, but it is too simple. What about weight loss? If you want to lose weight, then burn more calories than you consume. Profound, I know. We don't like the real solutions because they require change…and not minimal change—dramatic life change. The path to real results is simple but never easy.

The interesting thing is that we don't stop with finances and weight loss. We carry this same attitude into how we relate to God. We consume Jesus-junk and deny every thought of sacrifice. Jesus was clear when He said that we must die to self in order to follow Him. Bloated church consumers cannot follow Jesus, and our religious charlatans continue to fatten them up for the day of slaughter. They provide program after program for consumption but never preach the reality of laying down one's life in order to take up one's cross to follow Jesus.

We crave this Jesus-junk stuff and cannot get enough. How many times does the same book need to be written? How many times does the same sermon have to be preached? It is a never-ending cycle because just like the seven-minute abs, this consumer-driven spiritual stuff doesn't work!

Consumeranity will be revealed for the fraud that it is. It is a cheap expression of selfishness that requires little to nothing of those within its grasp. It is not built on the foundation of Christ and will therefore not stand the test of time. It is death waiting to be revealed.

The solution is simple, but it is not easy. Simply changing our programs, mission statements, leadership structures and orders of service will not fix a thing. It is not enough to change our outward appearance. A transformation must occur. An inside out transformation is needed. A complete metamorphosis is required. Consumerism must be pushed out, and we must return to the centrality of Christ and His mission.

Following Jesus is simple. Religious people tend to balk at simplicity. Religion relies on complexity. Keep it complex and confusing so that you are dependent upon the religious experts to feed you. They say, "You can't possibly understand this, so we will feed you a steady diet of religious junk food to keep you coming back for more."

Some will argue that simple is shallow. Consumeranity loves that argument. Consumeranity preachers talk a lot about being deep. They have "in-depth" Bible studies that are loaded with Bible trivia and arguments over debatable minutia. "Did Adam have a belly button?" "Numerology in scripture…the Bible code decoded." "What Jesus really meant to say."

Simple is not shallow, and complex is not deep. In fact, simplicity allows for maximum depth. Drilling into the basic, simple truths of following Jesus unlocks the pathway for tremendous relational depth. Complexity spreads us thin and provides excuses for ignoring God's voice. Consumers of religion cannot possibly understand the beauty of knowing Jesus and introducing Him to others.

Remember the church is not a building, a set of programs or a pastoral staff. The church is the Body of Christ. In order to carry out His mission, we must return to Christ and allow Him to remove every false pretense we have hitched ourselves to. Jesus can refine us, but we must understand that the purification process will burn. Are you willing to open yourself up to that process? Are you willing to feel the burn?

Scripture tells us that faith is being sure of what we hope for and certain of what we cannot see. What is it that you are hoping for? Is your primary hope for a pain-free life on easy street? Are your prayers riddled with demands for personal prosperity, promotion and protection? Guard your heart against Consumeranity and be certain that your hope is not misplaced. When our hope is squarely placed on carrying out the mission of Christ, we are assured great faith. It is a faith that we will lay down our lives for.

If your faith has cost you nothing, it is probably worthless. Nobody shares a worthless faith.

Do you have faith? What has it cost you? What is it worth? Is it worth sharing?

ISMs

ism *noun* \ˈi-zəm\
a belief, attitude, style, etc., that is referred to by a word
that ends in the suffix -ism
1. a distinctive doctrine, cause or theory
2. an oppressive and especially discriminatory attitude
   or belief

(Merriam-Webster.com 2014)

Who am I? What am I supposed to do? These are two of the primary questions that drive the human experience. The journey of life raises these questions on a consistent and steady basis. Navigating life is a difficult process. Without the proper tools and direction, it is easy to become lost amidst a landscape cluttered with opposing philosophies and ideologies. A seemingly infinite number of isms beg for our devotion and promise to provide the meaning we desperately desire.

All of us will give our lives to something. Some spend their earthly existence in the pursuit of wealth and possessions. Others take a nobler approach and dedicate themselves to various humanitarian efforts. For many, life is a vehicle for building a family and the home front drives their existence. Others seek fulfillment in careers and personal achievement. Ultimately these efforts leave us empty and wondering because they do not contain the purpose our Creator instilled deep within us.

Even the most successful is left to question: Who am I? What am I supposed to do?

All of our efforts come up short of the divine plan for life. The grand frustration found at the core of the search for significance leaves most stagnated in "survival mode" as true life passes by. They are just trying to make it through another day. They have no real purpose or direction.

Various forms of self-medication are employed to cope with the doldrums of merely existing and never truly living. Addictions, drugs, alcohol, sexual conquests, fantasy and various other coping mechanisms are utilized in vain efforts to simply make it through another day. Wandering aimlessly through life leaves you lost with no visible landmarks to help you navigate your way home.

The first seven years of my life where spent in a small, central Texas town. The town was peaceful and easy-going. It was the kind of place where you felt safe. Doors were left unlocked, and children could freely roam the neighborhood streets in carefree play. There were trees to climb, expanses to cross, people to see…it was a world of experience waiting to be discovered. It was not unusual for my sister and me to leave our childhood home for hours at a time to explore the parameters of our existence. It felt like we roamed for miles, but I am certain we always remained in a relative close proximity of home. I know this because we were always within earshot of my father's whistle. Dad would whistle when it was time to come home, and no matter where we were, we could always hear his call.

I can remember being caught up in the business of play… oblivious to the passage of time and movement of my surroundings as is common in childhood innocence. It was easy to forget where I was and how I got there, but my father's whistle always broke through the mist of my own imagination to draw me back to reality. His call was a grounding force in understanding my identity. Dad's whistle always created a chain reaction of thought. It went something like this:

> *"What's that sound? I know that sound. It's a whistle. Not just any whistle though. That's my whistle. What does it mean? Oh yeah, it means that it is time to come home. I have to go."*

In essence, my father's call would cause me to ask the two great questions: Who am I and what am I supposed to do? Back then the answers came easy. I was Bo Chancey, son of Mike Chancey, and I was supposed to go home. The only thing to do next was to figure out exactly where I was so that I could set the course for home. Fortunately I knew the lay of the land, and landmarks to determine my exact location were numerous.

There was the tree in middle of the road,
the house with the red door,
the water tower on the horizon,
the yard that was never mowed,
the backyard with three dogs,
the broken mailbox,
the orange Corvette,
the chimney painted black,
the dewberry bushes,
the dog with one blue eye,
Emory's house,
the big house with the swimming pool,
the gravel road,
the chain-link fence,
the big tree my kite got stuck in,
the little tree I ran into with my bike,
the old man on the porch,

the fork in the road,
and countless others.

All of them marked the path back to where I belonged…they showed me the way home.

Rockdale, Texas in the 1970s was a pretty uncomplicated place to navigate, but times change. My family moved to a suburb of Dallas.

There was more to do and more to see. Safety became an issue and doors had to be locked. Parameters were marked out around the family home. We could not explore beyond those boundaries. It became more difficult to hear my father's call above the noise of more cars, more people and more distractions. The pace of life was faster, and change was sudden. Landmarks changed daily. There were very few constants to help me navigate this vast new world.

The ease and simplicity of my childhood gave way to the storms of adolescence, the struggle toward adulthood, the new discovery of self and the burden of achievement. With each passing year, the answers to the two great questions became less and less clear and more and more complicated. Who was I and what was I supposed to do?

That is the nature of living. Progress and the pursuit of more carry us farther from home than we ever intended. It is quite normal to wake up one day with the shocking realization that you are utterly lost. You have no idea who you are or where you are going. You simply wander with a dim recollection of a secure identity and a long lost home. The familiar sound of your Father's call faintly rings in your ears, but you cannot identify the landmarks needed to navigate your way home. So you wander and wonder…"Who am I and what am I supposed to do?"

You were created to have a relationship with God. The Creator determines the purpose of His creation, and God's purpose for you is to be intimately united to Him. The meaning of life is a relatively simple thing when considered in this regard. Most people want to think that they have the right or ability to set the meaning of their life, but that search always leads to frustration when nothing is ever fully satisfying. No matter what you accomplish or achieve, there always remains a longing for more. Inner peace and identity acceptance are never achieved until we acquiesce to God's meaning for life.

Little kids do not have the hang ups that adults do. For the most part, they are not worried, stressed out or anxious. Status, appearance and individuality are not issues. They possess a simple willingness to just be who they are and enjoy whatever the day might hold. But something always shatters the innocence of childhood, and we are thrust headlong into the desperate search for the meaning of life.

Sin is the culprit. Consciousness of sin rips the secure identity of childhood out of our grasp and leaves us to question who we are. That is exactly what happened to Adam and Eve. They went from just being in the garden and enjoying the presence of God to the realization that they were naked, to looking for significance in labor (both work and childbirth) and to seeking to reconnect with God. Sin messed it all up for them, and it messes it all up for us. You will never discover any form of authentic peace in this world apart from reconnecting with God.

God is calling us home to Him. His call says, "You are Mine…you belong with Me…find your completeness in Me."

God is calling. It is time to go home. Do you know the way?

Do you have the answers to life's great questions?

Who am I? Why am I alive? What is the meaning of life?

These primary questions of identity are a haunting part of the human condition. We long for reason, purpose and destiny. The sum total of life's events must add up to something of value.

The notion that life is a series of random of events leading toward perpetual nothingness produces a hopelessness that runs counter to human nature.

People require hope.

There is short-term hope. We hope we get a good night's sleep. We hope to wake in the morning. We hope the car will start, traffic will be light and we will arrive at work on time. We hope to make it through the day without incident. We hope our families are well. We hope for leisurely distractions to captivate our attention. We hope our minds are settled enough to allow for sleep. Then we hope to do it all again.

Hope in the daily grind is less than satisfactory. We desire more, and the pursuit of long-term hope becomes paramount. A structured method of thinking and defining of self provide an illusion of order to the seemingly chaotic nature of being. The adoption of an ism creates a primary thread running through the narrative of life to hold the story together.

When we reject or neglect a relationship with God, isms become the foundation of existence. They are baseline thought processes that determine actions and measure relative success. Isms provide goals and structured reality. The perceived parameters of isms allow for life to be neatly ordered and maintained. We permit others who share a particular ism with us to inhabit the friendly confines of our world, while those who reject that ism are segregated outside the walls of our reality.

Cue the hostility.

Competing isms make relationships brutally challenging. Liberalism battles conservatism. Humanism opposes individualism. Legalism fights relativism. Socialism clashes with consumerism.

Isms divide.

There are isms for just about everything, and if you do not know what your isms are, you can simply invent a new ism. Think about your isms. What are the primary beliefs that define your existence?

Here are some examples to get you thinking:
Materialism
Intellectualism
Individualism
Consumerism
Familyism
Professionalism
Legalism
Nationalism
Liberalism
Conservatism
Humanism

If you struggle to find the proper isms to describe your primary existence, then simply add "ism" to the end of any word that represents your foundational identity.

We hold to a system of isms that work like intersecting circles to determine primary identity. Think about your top three isms. What are they?

Write them into the circles below.

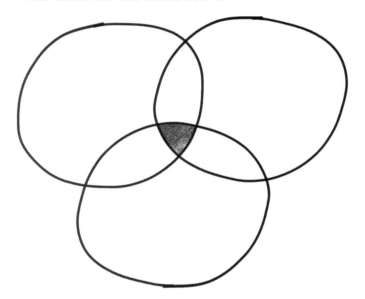

The shaded section where the three isms intersect is your fortress. This is the place you retreat to when threatened. It is your epicenter of belief, and it gives you a way to understand the world around you. The small percentage of people who share your sliver of belief are friends. The remainders are foes.

Isms produce schisms in humanity. People are divided and isolated. We attack other isms to justify our own. The battle lines are drawn, and war is waged.

We fight a civil war on false fronts while the real enemy reaps destruction undisturbed.

For our struggle is not against flesh and blood, but against the rulers, against the authorities, against the powers of this dark world and against the spiritual forces of evil in the heavenly realms.

Ephesians 6:12 (NIV)

Humanity does have an enemy, but it is not man himself. There is nothing right about the hostility we feel toward one another. As long as humankind is divided and fighting with itself, we will never be able to defeat the evil that plagues us.

Religion adds fuel to the fire. Our religious isms define and divide. Instead of drawing people into community built on the shared human experience, religion separates who is in and who is out and pits the ins and outs against one another. There are even schisms within religions. In order to further divide and fight, men create religious sects and denominations.

People are prone to label, attack and kill anything they do not understand. If something is outside of their isms, they feel threatened and bunker down in their fortresses. Holy wars commence, but there is nothing holy about war. Humanity's infighting grieves the heart of the Creator. God longs to reconcile all people into His family, but the isms are in the way.

Isms must die in order for us to understand the life God intends for us to possess. But remember that isms do not give rise to a physical, intellectual or emotional battle. The battle that rages in the core identity of every human being is a spiritual one.

When we allow isms instead of the Creator to define us, then our misunderstanding of who we are leads to all manner of unholy activity. All of the horrible things people do to one another can be traced directly back to one ism or another. The mixtures of various

isms that make up individuals' core identities are potent cocktails that produce vicious attacks.

Sadly, much of what is referred to as Christianity is not immune to the plague of isms infesting humanity. Denominationalism is a prime example. This particular ism has served Satan well. Denominations divide the Body of Christ based on preferred methodology, petty disagreements regarding nonessential matters and arrogance that promotes self-righteousness over biblical unity. When the Christians divide and fight with one another, Satan is the only one who wins. Consider all of the energy and resources expended fighting battles to defend isms within Christianity. What if those resources had been allocated where they belonged? The world would be a much different place. The mission of Jesus to save the world would have advanced more rapidly.

So, what is the deal? Why have Christian leaders allowed isms to infiltrate their ranks?

It is the draw of religion. Religion creates systems that can be navigated, manipulated and controlled. Again, denominationalism is a perfect example. At its core, denominationalism (along with every ism) is about power. "Our way is right, so align yourselves under our authority to believe and do what we say."

So, is non-denominationalism the answer? No…it is just another ism that combines with other isms to fight battles against even more isms.

Consider some of the isms that infect Christianity and knock churches off of their primary mission.

Racism. I know, I know…people in the United States do not believe racism exists anymore since we had a black President, but come on…our churches reveal another story. We have white churches, black churches, Hispanic churches, Asian churches and so on. How in the world could the church be the most racially segregated element of American society? If Sunday morning worship is any reflection of heaven, then one would have to imagine a very different heaven than what is depicted in the Bible. Christians should be cultural leaders in the expulsion of racism; instead, we continue to be some of the worst offenders.

My friends, this should not be.

Intellectualism. This is "the smarter you are, the more righteous you are" line of thinking. Religion thrives on intellectualism because it creates a system that is dependent upon experts. The experts are the most formally educated, and they actively perpetuate a culture that benefits the intellectual elite. Complex systems of thought are developed and "deep" teaching is primarily peripheral nonsense that has nothing to do with Christ's primary agenda. The Pharisees of Jesus' day could fall into this category. Jesus condemned them for weighing people down with burdens they could not carry. Churches that do not make the simple truths of Jesus accessible to everyone because of intellectualism have wandered from their primary purpose.

My friends, this should not be.

Nationalism. This is a dicey one because nationalism generally contains a variety of other isms. In the United States, it is often a mixture of capitalism, isolationism and patriotism. A Christian mindset help captive by nationalism struggles to perceive what God is doing on a grander scale. In the United States, there is often an underlying belief that "Christian" and "American" are almost synonymous. The primary thought then would be that whatever is best for my nation is what God desires. Nationalism and Christianity do not always run contrary to one another, but at some point they will diverge. What happens when an American value runs contrary to Jesus? Who wins? More often than not, Jesus will be distorted to fit nationalism.

My friends, this should not be.

There is a better way. When we understand what isms we adhere to, then we are able to recognize when they begin to overtake our relational identity in God's family. Isms must be put to death daily in order to fully enjoy the wondrous adventure of building God's kingdom.

Isms cannot provide the answers we are looking for.

Who am I?

What am I supposed to do?

What is my primary purpose?

A relationship with Jesus answers these and all of life's great questions. Never exchange the beauty of a dynamic relationship with the living God for the shallow answers of isms. Isms produce schisms. The most deadly schism of all is the isms that separate us from God. Jesus came and died for all humankind so that we could be free to leave the fortress of our isms behind. In Christ, isms are no longer needed.

Jesus is our identity.

Jesus is our refuge.

Jesus is our answer.

LIFE

Lord Lord, yes indeed
If you're my Lord then here's my needs

I want some of this and some of that
Let's get this going. I need it stat

Sure sure, I'll follow you
I'll do anything you want me to

Within reason, don't get carried away
Lordship's not literal, it's just something to say

Blank blank, I'll do anything but
Take a step out of my religious rut

My blanks keep me safe and sound
Praying in circles round and round

– Shiloh Battles

DYING TO LIVE

My earliest memory is of the rear bumper of a 1977 Cadillac coming at my head.

Mom and Dad were working, and I was at my babysitter's house for the day. I was playing with a toy car…pushing it down the sidewalk in front of the house. I stopped at the neighbor's driveway and watched as the lady who lived there rushed out to her car to run an errand. The driveway was on an incline and she did not notice me kneeling on the sidewalk. She backed out in a hurry and cut the wheel a bit too sharply causing the rear end to come right at my head.

There was nothing I could do. I could not move. There was not even time to scream. I simply remember looking up and seeing that bumper coming at me. I closed my eyes and prayed, "Okay, God."

That is my first memory. What I remember next was that there was peace. Everything went black, and I had a floating sensation. Believe it or not…I saw a light, and it felt like I was moving toward the light. It was warm.

Then I screamed.

The peace was gone. I do not remember feeling pain, but I was so afraid.

That is what I remember.

This is what I was told happened. The bumper hit me and knocked me backwards. The rear tire grabbed my left leg and pulled me under. (To this day, I have a massive scar on my left thigh from where the tire burned me.) My neck was caught in the car's suspension spring. I swallowed my tongue and could not breathe.

The driver felt the car hit me, so she slammed on the brakes and put it in park. When she realized that she had run over a child, she ran into her house to get her husband. Her husband had some training in lifesaving, and he instructed her to call an ambulance while he jumped into action. He removed my neck from the spring and pulled the car off of me. I was not breathing, so he began CPR.

I was in bad shape. All the blood vessels in my face had broken, so my face was purple and my eyes were filled with blood. They said that I was legally dead at one point and resuscitated. The ambulance arrived and took me to a local hospital where my dad caught up to us. From there I was transported to a larger hospital about 45 minutes away. My dad was with me in the ambulance, and I remember crying. Dad asked me why I was crying, and I told him that it was because my stomach hurt. He told me that if I stopped crying my stomach would stop hurting.

So, I stopped crying.

They would not let me go to sleep. I wanted to sleep so badly. I just wanted to close my eyes and experience peace. Not a chance.

They were concerned that I might not regain consciousness, so they would not allow me to close my eyes. Dad kept talking to me.

My mom was working in a neighboring town and was driving by herself to the big hospital to meet us. She had a long drive with no information and nobody to talk to. All she knew was that a car had hit me and that it was bad. There were no cell phones. She drove and prayed. What do you pray in that situation? She essentially prayed, "Okay, God."

I spent three days in ICU and a week in the hospital. Nothing was broken, but I looked terrible. The tire burn covered my entire left thigh. My face was a scary mess. I remember very little from the hospital except being lowered into a whirlpool bath. The warm water felt like thousands of needles were being jabbed into my leg where the tire burn was.

I almost never tell this story. I tried it once in a sermon, and I remember that about halfway through, the tension was so great I said, "It's okay…I lived." I do not like to tell this story because it is so personal. It is my story.

It is hard to see the eyes roll when I say that I saw a bright light. Believe me…I know it is cliché. I do not like all the detail-oriented questions that I just do not know the answers to. It is what I remember from a four-year-old perspective combined with details that my parents provided over the years.

It is strange when your first memory is of dying. I feel as though I have this experiential understanding of death that is difficult to put into words. I know that death is not the end. I know it. It is not that I have faith or believe it…I know it.

Being hit by that car changed everything. It is a part of my identity that I am reminded of every time I look at or touch my left leg. I was dead, but before I died I prayed, "Okay, God."

And it was okay. And it will be okay. I know it.

When we would visit my grandparents in the small Oklahoma town where they lived, I loved to sit at the dining room table with my grandmother. She was a tough old broad with a perpetual twinkle in her eye that informed you that her mind was sharp. She was calm and one of the coolest people I have ever known. She spent most of her time listening and learning, but when she spoke, there was wisdom and power. She chose her words carefully and said them with a graciousness that seems lost to a bygone era.

I would sit next to her and gently play with the loose skin on the top of her hand. There was something magically cathartic about pulling the skin up and watching is return to its smooth position. When the room would empty and it was quiet and still, she would turn to me and speak words of life. She would say, "God has big plans for you. I have known it since you were four years old."

I understood what she meant, and she had no intention of letting me ever forget it. There is gravity as well as hope in those words. There is an understanding that squandering my life is not an acceptable option. I am alive because God wanted me to be alive. My life is not my own. My grandmother told me so.

When you are given a second chance at life, there are expectations that you do something valuable with it. It is not to be wasted on frivolous matters. Second chance living creates a world view filled with intentionality and purpose.

A relationship with Jesus gives us a second chance at life, but there is dying that needs to be done. In order to relationally follow Jesus, we must die to self. New life is birthed through the death of the old self.

Jesus said that in order to follow Him we must first lay down our lives and take up our crosses. The eternal life found in Jesus cannot be received without death. We lay down our lives just as Jesus laid down His. We surrender our will for a better Way.

This is hard, and Jesus knows it. Jesus came from heaven to earth for the purpose of saving humankind. He was born to die. That was the plan, but when the time came for the dying to occur, Jesus had some questions.

The night Jesus was arrested before His crucifixion, He prayed alone in the Garden of Gethsemane. He cried out to the Father to find out if there was another way. The scriptures say that Jesus prayed earnestly to the point where His sweat became like drops of blood. Jesus agonized over what the Father wanted Him to do.

But He prayed, "Not my will but yours be done." He said, "Okay, God."

When Jesus left the garden, He was resolute. The time had come for the dying to begin. Judas' kiss kicked off the festivities. Peter drew his sword and was ready to fight, but Jesus had no intention of fighting flesh and blood battles. He willingly went with the soldiers and marched to His death.

Jesus laid down His life. It was not taken from Him. He died on purpose for a purpose.

The same Jesus who walked on water, healed the sick, fed the hungry and raised the dead could have escaped or called down fire from heaven, but instead He submitted Himself to death on a cross.

It was brutal.

There was intense physical pain. In addition to the beating He endured and the nails driven through His hands and feet, crucifixion brought death through asphyxiation. Jesus had to push up on the nails through His feet in order to get air into His lungs. Eventually there was a decision not to push up anymore, and Jesus breathed His last.

There was emotional pain. Jesus loved the people who crucified Him. He cried out to His Father, "Forgive them for they know not what they do." Jesus saw His friends and even His mother at the foot of the cross. He was mocked and ridiculed by the crowd who came to witness the spectacle of His death.

The physical and emotional pain were nothing compared to the spiritual pain. When Jesus breathed His last, He called out in a loud voice, "My God, my God, why have you forsaken me?" It was a cry of tremendous spiritual pain. This was the moment that Jesus received the sin of humanity onto Himself, and that sin brought separation from His Father. He had never experienced sin and had never been relationally separated from the Father. Death was new to Jesus, and it hurt.

But His death was not the end. New life came through the resurrection, and we are invited to live again with Jesus. Christianity hinges on the reality of the resurrection, but the resurrection could not take place without the crucifixion. Death comes before life in a relationship with Jesus. We share in His death so that we are free to experience the abundant life He promises through His resurrection.

Faith in Jesus declares that the old self is dead and gone and the new self is alive and eternal. Jesus was crystal clear about what following Him would entail. He knows our propensity to believe self-centered lies, and He strongly stated the truth. Jesus said that in order to follow Him we must lay down our lives and take up our crosses. It is impossible to follow Jesus without first dying to self and then doing it again and again and again. We carry crosses because dying to self is not a one-time event…it is a daily occurrence.

When we refuse to die to self, it is impossible to follow Jesus.

Consider the biblical story about the rich young ruler. A man who had wealth, youth and power came to Jesus and asked what he must do to inherit eternal life. Jesus essentially told the man to obey the Old Testament Law. The man boldly declared that he had kept the Law since he was a boy, but Jesus told him that he still lacked one thing.

The one thing that he lacked is the one thing we all lack. It is an identity issue. Who we were is put to death so that we can be alive through a relationship with Jesus. This man had a lot going for him. He had youth, wealth and power. Jesus told him to go sell his possessions, give the proceeds to the poor and then follow Him. Essentially Jesus told the man that he had to have a new identity. He could not be the rich young ruler any longer. He must die to self before he could ever follow Jesus.

Jesus' command was not meant to be a burden. It was a blessing. Jesus offered the rich young ruler a new life through a relationship with Him, but the cost was more than the man was willing to pay. His face fell because he had great wealth. The cost of following Jesus was more than he was willing to pay.

The rich young ruler walked away. He did not say, "Okay, God."

And Jesus did not chase him.

Jesus did not call out and attempt to renegotiate the deal. Jesus did not make another offer. He did not say, "Okay…I understand that selling everything is a bit extreme. Let's meet somewhere in the middle. Go sell half your possessions. No? Still too much? How about a third of your possessions? Work with me pal. I'm trying to help."

Jesus did not do that because He was not trying to make a deal. Jesus was telling the truth. There was no way that man could follow Him without first dying to self. The rich young ruler needed to lay down his identity. He had to give up his youth, wealth and power in order to receive new life through a relationship with Jesus. He lacked one thing. He had to die to self.

Jesus then shocked the people who witnessed His encounter with the rich young ruler by saying that it is easier for a camel to pass through the eye of a needle than for a rich man to enter the kingdom of heaven. The people asked who could possibly be saved. Jesus said, "It is impossible for man, but with God all things are possible."

It is possible for everyone to be saved, but not without dying to self first. We cannot share in Jesus' resurrection until we share in His death. In order to receive new life, the old life must pass away. Whatever we were without Jesus is crucified with Christ. In essence, we put it all on the table. We go and sell all of our possessions. Then we are free to follow Jesus. Then we have new life.

New life comes with expectations.

It is not to be squandered. It is a gift from God that is intended to be used for His glory. The beauty of a relationship with

Jesus is that we are far more than recipients of His kingdom—we are participants in building His kingdom. We are given new life so that we can live abundantly.

Abundant living is found through daily dying to self and actively pursuing Jesus. It is no walk down easy street. Following Jesus is a treacherous and wild adventure. It is rarely tiptoeing through the tulips but is more often a stumbling journey of epic proportions. Pain avoidance cannot be a primary thought process. Our goal is not to enter into heaven smelling of roses but to stumble into eternity battered, bruised and dragging as many people with us as possible.

I love the story of Lazarus. Lazarus was dead. He was a rotting corpse when Jesus called him out of his tomb. Can you imagine? There was Lazarus—wrapped in grave clothes, flesh decaying, dead and gone. But Jesus decided that Lazarus' story would not end in death. Jesus stood outside His friend's tomb and called out, "Lazarus, come out!"

Out he came. That had to be a freaky moment. I probably would have screamed at the sight of a dead guy cruising out of his tomb all wrapped up like a mummy. Were the people there thinking that the Zombie Apocalypse had begun? Those people knew Lazarus was dead. They were the ones who prepared his body for burial and put him in the tomb a few days earlier.

Then Jesus declared, "Take off the grave clothes and let him go!" Jesus told them to take off that death because he was alive. That is exactly what Jesus is telling all of us today. He proclaims that we are free to step out of death, to take off the old self so that we can live with Him.

Lazarus lived, and he had an amazing story to tell. Every time he met people and said his name, he was probably asked the same thing, "Wait…are you that Lazarus?" Every time he went to a party, he probably heard, , "Hey, Lazarus, tell everyone about that time you died and rose again." Lazarus had a new identity. He was the guy who died and lived again.

So many people believed in Jesus because of Lazarus that Jesus' opponents were making plans to kill him as well as Jesus. Do you think that worried Lazarus? I don't. He had to be thinking, "I've been dead before and Jesus handled it…if they want to kill me again, I think I'll be okay."

What about you? Are you alive or dead? Have you received new life from Jesus?

If so, new life comes with expectations. If you say, "Okay, God," then you have a story to tell. You have a life to live. You have a mission from God. God has big things in store for you!

GREY MATTER

I f life is only black and white, why did God give us grey matter?

I look at it this way, but you don't agree.
Whose view is better? About that we will see.

I can't be wrong. There's no way that you're right.
So proceed to disagree and put up your fight.

I look at it this way. It's the way it must be.
You can't see that, so you're dead to me.

You're a ghost, an illusion, a vapor, a mist.
You have no substance. You do not exist.

I look at is this way. Period. The end.
My mind is made up. My will will not bend.
                                        – Shiloh Battles

Religion has all the answers. Relationships ask better questions.

I am always leery of a church that has an eight-page doctrinal statement. They have simply figured out way too much of God for my liking. There is no mystery, no wonderment and no room for disagreement.

A religious system is dependent on having everything figured out. It needs black and white answers to every question in order to maintain structure and hierarchy. Opposing viewpoints are shut down with forceful rhetoric and standardized responses. The Bible is often abused to prove points instead of used to encounter the living God.

It should be obvious that God does not intend for us to figure Him out and wrap Him up in neat little packages with pretty bows on top. Brilliant scholars and theologians who are filled with evidence of the Holy Spirit have disagreed on all kinds of peripheral doctrine for centuries. They read the same texts, love the same God and want the same things but wind up at opposing ends of the spectrum. Why?

The "why" is simple. Jesus did not come to create a new religion. He came to invite all people into a relationship with Him. Religion is neat and tidy, but relationships are messy.

Religion's first response is "no." "No, you can't do that. No, you can't say that. No, you can't think that. No, you can't challenge that."

Relationship's first response is "yes." "Yes, I see why you would do that. Yes, I understand what you are saying. Yes, we should think about that together. Yes, of course you can challenge that."

Religion shuts people down, but relationship builds everyone up. People are indoctrinated into religion and invited into relationship. Would you rather indoctrinate people or invite people? Would you rather argue to prove points about God or invite others to discover the unchanging yet ever-revealing Living God of the Universe?

When we deny people the opportunity to discover, we deny the essential nature of Jesus. The four gospels are centered on the relational nature of Jesus. He said things like "come and see," "follow me," "I'm going to your house today," "in my Father's house are many rooms…I am going there to prepare a place for you" and "apart from me you can do nothing." The religious-minded people of Jesus' day had no framework to process what He said. In their minds, Jesus' words ran contrary to their life's devotion. Their inability or refusal to think prevented them from knowing Jesus.

Our God is a relational God. He is relational to His very core. He created humankind to be in relationship with Him. God walked with Adam and Eve in the garden. He engaged Adam in the work of creation by having Adam name the animals. God needs nothing, but He desires relationship with us. His heart was broken when Adam and Eve chose rebellion over relationship.

Religion is often just another gussied-up version of rebellion. It breaks God's heart when we choose religion over relationship.

I am fortunate to live in the most irreligious state in the USA. This context provides freedom to thoughtfully explore the relational nature of God and His desire for people to connect to Him. The religious culture in other parts of the country can be so stifling that there is no space for thoughtful dialogue. Legitimate questions are shot down with rote responses. Religion perceives questions as an attack that must be thwarted. People are shot down and defeated instead of embraced and encouraged. Religion fights against people who do not believe, but relationship fights for and with people who do not believe.

An example of this can be seen in the statement Jesus made in John 14. Jesus said, "I am the way, the truth and the life. No one comes to the father except through me." Jesus claims exclusivity. This is a huge statement with grand implications. It is crucial that we understand the difficulty many people have with this foundational thought.

Most people want to believe that all paths lead to heaven or at the very least that many paths lead there. The statement that Jesus is the only way rightly disturbs them. It is imperative that we allow people space to process and think through concepts that run contrary to their current world views. Far too often, we put needless barriers to meeting Jesus in people's paths. We argue from a defensive posture instead of reasoning alongside them. We draw imaginary lines in sand, stand on the other side and demand that people make a leap of faith. There is a better way. Enter into a person's world, lock arms with him or her and take logical steps of faith as you journey together toward Jesus.

In sharing the exclusive claim of Jesus, I typically say something like this: "Jesus said that He is the way, the truth and the life and that no one comes to the Father except through Him. Many people find that statement disturbing and I totally understand that thought process. We want to believe that all or many paths lead to heaven because the thought of anyone not being in heaven is gut-wrenching. That feeling is right in line with the heartbeat of God. He can't stand the thought of anyone not being in His heavenly home for all of eternity. If I knew 52 ways to get to heaven, I would share all 52 with you. I would make an interactive road map of all the paths so that you could choose your own adventure, but I don't know 52 ways…I know one way. God revealed one way to Him, and that way is through Jesus. Jesus came to earth to put our sins to death in His body so that we could share in His resurrection. No other pathway or religion makes provision for the removal of sin. It is easy to be irritated at God for only making one way, but in that moment we forget that He made a WONDERFUL way. For God so loved us that He gave His one and only Son so that whoever believes in Him will not perish, but have everlasting life! God made a way, and no matter what you've done or what's been done to you, you are invited to come to God through that Way... through Jesus."

You cannot give someone directions until you know where they are coming from. Speak less. Listen more. Enter into someone's world and don't get your wheels shot off every time someone challenges one of your foundational truths. If you allow space for questions and thoughtful wrestling, you will discover the joy of engaging relationally with God and people.

There are absolute truths...of this I am absolutely sure, but there is also a space between that must be explored. Leaving the security of our clearly defined beliefs to explore the grey matters is a wonderful adventure that produces eternal results. Step into the grey matter and invite others to leave their side to explore with you. This neutral territory allows for meaningful discussion and heart-wrenching honesty. It is cruel to deny people the opportunity to wrestle with and question a new world view before asking them to adopt it.

There are also relative truths—of this I am absolutely sure—relatively speaking.

It is interesting when we find absolute and relative truths regarding the same thing. For instance, the temperature of a room might be 72 degrees Fahrenheit. We could look at a thermometer and know with absolute certainty that the temperature in the room is 72 degrees Fahrenheit. That would be an absolute truth, but there would also be relative truths based on individual experiences.

Is 72 degrees Fahrenheit hot, cold, warm, cool or just right? It depends on the individual and any number of variables he/she may be experiencing. So, it may be 72 degrees Fahrenheit (an absolute truth) and someone may say they are cold (a relative truth). It would be extremely foolish to argue with someone about whether they are feeling hot or cold. First of all, you cannot possibly know what they feel, and secondly, their relative experience may be different from yours.

They may have walked into the room from a snowstorm while you were sitting by the fire for three hours. They feel cold and you feel hot. Who is right and who is wrong? Both are right and neither is wrong.

The reality is that people experience absolute truths in relative ways. Our relative experiences do not alter the absolute truth, but they do produce spaces of grey matter where we can engage relationally with others to connect in powerful ways.

Somewhere along the way, many Christians became fearful of grey matters. A simple study of the book Acts reveals that the early church embraced thoughtful discussion and meaningful dialogue. Early church leaders were not afraid to enter into public spaces to reason with people. They were not separatists who isolated themselves from the world Jesus charged them to reach. They were bold and fearlessly shared the love of Jesus in thoughtfully engaging ways. They were not street-corner preachers who wasted breath screaming culturally irrelevant words to the sky. They actually understood their cultural context and loved the people enough to enter their worlds in order to engage them on a thoughtful journey.

When I was a student at Texas A&M University, a friend and I decided that we wanted to attend the Atheist/Agnostic Club on campus. At that time, the club was small and did not have much of a presence at the university. Our initial thought process was that we would show up and WIN them all to Christ. We were on a mission, but God had other plans.

The first Tuesday night that we attended the Atheist/Agnostic Club was eye opening to say the least. My buddy and I thoughtfully prepared all day. We were not thinking about how to lovingly enter into the world of others to listen and learn. We were thinking about which Christian T-shirts we should wear, which crosses to put around our necks and which Bibles to carry under our arms. These were big decisions for us. We wanted T-shirts that were bold and in your face…nothing soft and simple like the "Got God?" shirts that played off of the "Got Milk?" commercials of that time period. I went with a shirt that said, "I believe in the BIG BANG theory…God spoke and BANG it was!" My friend put on his trusty "Lord's Gym" shirt that had a picture of a muscle bound Jesus carrying a cross and the words "bench presses this" on the bottom. I chose a wooden cross to wear around my neck so as not to appear gaudy and my friend went with a James Avery silver cross with a black velvet necklace that really popped against the simple design of his shirt. We both carried our biggest, leather-bound NIV study Bibles, and off we went.

I will never forget walking into that classroom for the first time. There were about 20 people gathered and their cheery chatter came to a screeching halt as we arrogantly strutted through the door. All those eyes turned to us and most of them rolled. They had seen this type of thing before. There was a "here we go again" look about them. The president of the club walked over and introduced himself and welcomed us. There was a glint in his eye that communicated that he knew something that we did not. What he knew was how to handle people like us.

The group was nice enough in how they dealt with our invasion, but there was a hint of condescension in their speech. It turns out that several times each semester different Christians would show up and shout some turn or burn rhetoric then scurry back to their Bible study groups like they had just won a game of truth or dare. About the only thing we did right that night was to realize that we were in way over our heads, and we simply shut up and listened.

Then we went back the next week.

And the week after that.

And the week after that.

And the week after that.

We just kept showing up.

It was awesome. Before long the group opened up to us and dropped some of their defenses. We learned so much from a perspective our holy huddles could never provide. We did very little talking, and just about any point we would try to make was quickly put down with prepared arguments. The Atheist/Agnostic club knew the Bible better than any Christian group I had ever been a part of. Each week they met together to discuss different topics, but no matter what the topic was, they ended up discussing Christianity. They were like vegetarians who can't stop talking about meat.

At one point the president of the club told us that they were not like Christians because people who are drawn to Christianity have a need to be in community with like-minded people. His premise was that atheists and agnostics did not have that kind of need and therefor did not have to accept any kind of God. He failed to see the irony that he was president of a group of like-minded people who met together every week to form a stronger "church" than most churches I've ever encountered. It was a tight knit group, and their purpose was clear. They met together to strengthen their belief that Christianity was wrong.

I have no idea if my friend and I had a positive impact on the rest of the group, but the experience definitely helped us. Our eyes became open to a new way of looking at people and entering into their worlds. That kind of thinking is often absent from our churches today. We were reminded of the type of isolationist, fear-based thinking that consumes many Christians one day as we were walking across campus and met the president of a prominent Christian club.

My buddy and I randomly bumped into a couple of guys, and they asked if we were Christians. We told them we were, and they invited us to come to a Bible study. We asked when and where, and they said that it met on Tuesday nights. We told them that we were busy on Tuesday nights, and they responded with a typical religious guilt-inducing response by asking what could be more important than going to a Bible study. When we told them that we attended the Atheist/Agnostic club on Tuesday nights, you would have thought that we had the plague! Their eyes got wide, and the mouths dropped open. There was an uncomfortable silence that hung in the air until the president of the club informed us that going to the Atheist/Agnostic club was dangerous.

Dangerous? Really?

That guy proceeded to lecture us about how we could be led astray from faith in Jesus by hanging out with "those people." He was wrong. We continued to hang out with "those people," and our faith in Jesus was strengthened more through that experience than any Bible study I've ever been a part of.

It is sad that so many Christians are convinced that it is not okay to think, question and wrestle with different ideas. God has used my time with the Atheist/Agnostic group repeatedly over the years to remind me of the power of listening to people, understanding where they are coming from and engaging them in meaningful dialogue.

There are times when the best thing a Christian can do is to shut up and listen. Let your presence speak volumes. Stop trying to give directions to people when you have no idea where they are coming from. James 1:19 says, "My dear brothers and sisters, take note of this: Everyone should be quick to listen, slow to speak and slow to become angry." Anger is a common response to a perceived threat. People often get angry when their faith is challenged because they've been taught to fear that. We do not need to fear our faith being challenged. It is actually a faith-builder and ought to be embraced with great joy. Instead of being angry and disengaging, we have the freedom to ask clarifying questions in order to understand the challenge.

We do not have a blind faith. We have faith that is based on evidence and the realness of God. Since it is not a blind faith, we should allow others to investigate and search with freedom and grace. Christians should encourage questions and challenges to faith. It is a wonderful thing when our cultural rises up and thoughtfully says, "Hey, wait a minute...we aren't sure we are picking up what you are throwing down."

Christian leaders need to stop getting their underwear in a bunch every time they are challenged. Religion works on a hierarchal system that answers questions with "Because I said so."

Christianity is not a religion, so our answer needs to be relationally driven. Enter into a person's world in order to help him/her experience an absolute truth in a different way.

Engage your mind. Have a thoughtful faith. Learn to ask better questions. And by all means, do not fear the grey matter. The grey matter is where faith multiplies and initiates thoughtful, loving action.

Praying Blanks

When I was a kid, I saw a television ad for "Zips" tennis shoes. Zips were a new kind of shoe, and the ad grabbed my attention. It showed a kid who put on his brand new Zips then instantly began "zipping" around the room at lightning speed.

I was utterly enthralled. As a kid, I was not exactly what you would call "swift of foot." I was "big-boned" to put it mildly and a bit challenged in the zipping department. I had never won a race of any kind, and I desperately wanted those Zips tennis shoes.

I just knew that if I could get my feet into a pair of those shoes, I would be the fastest boy in school. I immediately asked my mother for a pair, but she easily rejected me by pointing out that she had just purchased me a new pair of Nikes.

Blasted! There was no way I was getting new shoes until those Nikes were worn out. I began scraping them with rocks, and I drug my toes everywhere I went in hopes that a hole would appear.

Each day I begged my mom for a new pair of Zips to no avail. Until one morning, out of the blue, my mom asked me if I still wanted a pair. Did I ever? She informed that she would pick me up from school that day, and we would go purchase some Zips.

Well, I was a new man. I walked into school that day with a confident swagger. I was about to be the fastest kid around, and I wanted everyone to know it. I walked right up to the undefeated racing champion of our second grade class. His name was Emory, and he was my best friend. I called him out, right there in front of everyone and challenged him to a race after school. He laughed at my challenge but still agreed to meet me in front of his house at 5:00p.m.

Little did he know that I would possess a secret weapon.

I will never forget how excited I was when my mother paid for the blue Zips with the white "Z" going down the side. My day had finally come.

I took the shoes home in their box because I did not want to waste any of their magical powers. I carried that box to Emory's house, and just before the race I carefully laced them up.

The anticipation rose as I stood poised at the starting line. A confident grin spread across my face as Emory's sister said, "On your mark, get set…Go!"

I burst off the starting line but quickly realized things were not as I thought they would be. The shoes did not work. Emory easily beat me. I was utterly crushed.

I went straight home, took off my new Zips, put them back in the box and shoved them under my bed. I was determined never to think of them again.

A few days passed, and my mom finally asked why I wasn't wearing the new shoes I had so desperately wanted. I informed her that they did not work.

"They didn't work?" she asked. "Did they not fit?"

"No, they fit," I said. "They just didn't work."

"Well did they hurt your feet?" mom asked.

"No, they just didn't work," I said.

"Did they not protect your feet against the elements?"

"No, mom, they just didn't work."

Mom couldn't understand. She purchased me shoes knowing full well what they were capable of doing, but I had another set of expectations that were unmet.

I think that most of us have done the same thing with Jesus. Jesus died on the cross so that we could follow Him and produce everlasting fruit, but we expect something different.

I have heard people say to me, "I tried praying, but it didn't work." What do you mean it didn't work? What were you expecting? If you think that God is your little Genie in a bottle, you are going to be disappointed. It won't work, but if God is your loving Savior who longs for you to know Him, prayer is a beautiful expression of a deep relationship.

Prayer is an opportunity to connect to the heartbeat of the living God. In prayer, we can hear from God and discover more of His majesty and grace. The purpose of prayer is not to convince God to do our will but to align our hearts and minds to His will. In order to experience the transformational power of prayer, everything must be made available to God.

Impotent prayer is filled with blanks.

But there is power in prayer.

There is power in prayer.

There is power in prayer.

Where is the power in prayer? Do you experience breakthroughs, revelations and miracles? Are your prayers filled with passionate expectation and glorious inspiration? When you pray, are you shaken to your very core and compelled to action?

If there is no power in your prayers, I suggest that you are doing it wrong. Relax…I know that I am not supposed to tell you that you are praying incorrectly, but for the love of God, isn't it time someone told the truth? There are right and wrong ways to pray. I am aware how the use of "right and wrong" shoots people's wheels off in our relative, everybody's right, nobody is wrong, make-sure-everybody-gets-a-trophy cultural context.

In the Sermon on the Mount, Jesus taught us how to pray. He said that there are wrong ways and right ways to pray.

When you pray, do not babble. You will not be heard because of your many words. Rambling on and on in prayer is a silly notion anyway. God already knows your heart. You are not telling Him anything new. Our words in prayer are merely a gateway to opening up our hearts to hear from God.

When you pray, do not do it to communicate anything to anyone but God. Prayer is not to be used to demonstrate our holiness, wisdom or knowledge. It is not intended for gossip or preaching.

When you pray, recognize who you are talking with. "Our Father in heaven, hallowed be your name." We are speaking with our Creator. His ways are higher than ours. He knows things we do not. He has perspective that we cannot see without Him. He is holy, righteous and powerful. The first order of prayer is to exalt God and humble self.

When you pray, seek God's will not your own. "Your kingdom come…your will be done…on earth as it is in heaven." We want God's kingdom not our kingdom. We want God's will not our will to be done. Why do we waste so much time and energy attempting to convince God to do our will when He longs to reveal His will to us?

When you pray, recognize what God promises and provides. "Give us this day our daily bread and forgive us our debts as we forgive our debtors." Forgiveness is as essential to life as daily bread. God provides for our basic needs but is not particularly interested making us fat, over-indulged spoiled brats. Daily bread is a reminder of God's faithfulness as a provider and our dependence upon Him. We need forgiveness just like we need daily bread, and God gives generously. We are then free to forgive as we are forgiven.

When you pray, remember who you are. "Lead us not into temptation, but deliver us from evil. For thine is the kingdom, the power and the glory forever. Amen." We are holy. We are set apart for the purpose of building God's kingdom with His power. The temptation of wasted living is to believe that this life is somehow about building our own personal kingdoms. We abuse God's power when we misuse our lives. His power transforms us and gives us new purpose. It is evil to refuse to yield to God's will.

Prayer is an opportunity to connect to the heartbeat of God. In prayer, we become aligned to God's will and are empowered by His Holy Spirit. Prayer is powerful because it changes us.

The problem with the way that most people pray is that they are not actually seeking God. Most people pray in ridiculous attempts to convince God to do their will. This nonsense is a pitiful substitute for genuine prayer and is taught to us out of the depths of Hell.

The lie that prayer is primarily a function of asking God to do things for us comes from a faulty foundational premise. It begins with our understanding of lordship.

Jesus is Lord.

Seriously…Jesus is Lord. He is THE Lord. Period. The end. Jesus is Lord.

His lordship is a fact. The variable is how you respond to the knowledge of that fact. You can live in a yielded state to His lordship. You can live in rebellion to His lordship. OR…you can take a hybrid approach by subtly perverting lordship with the seemingly harmless phrase, "Jesus is Lord of MY life."

It is a phrase that Christendom embraced in recent decades, but when combined with cultural norms such as consumerism and individualism, the power of true lordship is lost.

Think about it.

If Jesus is Lord of MY life, then what are the implications? Well…it is MY life and if He is going to be in charge, then I have some things that need taken care of. I want MY life to be the best life I can imagine. I'll readily admit that I have made a mess of my life, so I'm glad to have someone like Jesus to come in and make everything like I have always wanted.

"So…okay, Jesus…you can be Lord of My life and as such, I will consistently provide you with a list of my demands. Here are the things I need. Here are the things I want. Here are the things I need you to fix. Here are the things that are off limits. Here are the things I require for me to believe in you. Chop-chop, Jesus. Time is wasting. This is my one and only life, and I'm counting on you to make all my wildest dreams come true."

The problem with the "Lord of MY life" line of thinking is that in order to be a follower of Jesus, you must lay your life down. The principle requirement for following Jesus is dying to self. If you are a Christian, then there is no longer any "my life." There is only His life. We die to self and are raised into new life in Christ. The old has gone and the new has come. We are not our own but belong to Jesus. We are purchased by His blood and are slaves to Christ.

Prayer then is an opportunity to hear from God. If our prayers are primarily attempts to convince God to do our will, then we have lordship reversed. Why would I want God to do my will? That is foolish. What good is my will? I want His will to be done.

That is the power of prayer. Yielding to God's will and submitting yourself to Him is where His power is unleashed in your life. But nothing destroys the power of prayer faster than praying blanks.

"I'll do anything, but _____."

"I'll love anyone, but _____."

"I'll go anywhere, but _____."

"I'll give anything, but _____."

"I'll trust you with everything, but _____."

"I'll forgive everyone, but _____."

"I'll obey any command, but _____."

If you are praying blanks, you will not experience the fullness of God's miraculous power in your life. You will miss out on the abundant life Jesus promised. You will compartmentalize and attempt situational lordship. It will not work, and the consequences are eternal.

Yep. The stakes are that high. It is not an issue of your personal salvation. That is predicated on faith in Christ alone and the work He has done for you. I suppose one could pray blanks and still be saved, but there is far more at stake here.

It is not just about you. It is about your world. Your world is your home, your neighborhood, your community, your workplace and all the people you encounter. How is God using you to share His love in your world? This is why Lordship matters. Surrendering to God's will in prayer is crucial if you want to fully experience life in Christ.

Life in Christ is full of passionate sacrifice and joyful surrender. Life in Christ puts everything on the table and refuses to pray blanks.

"God, I will love anyone, go anywhere, give everything, trust you completely, forgive everyone and obey you fully." Imagine what God would do if you prayed like that.

Good intentions are not enough. Faithful action is required. That is the only way the lordship relationship can work.

I once had a staff member working for me who had a difficult time understanding the boss/employee relationship.

One of his responsibilities was paying the church's bills. We were running a simple office at the time, and there were only a few bills to pay...electricity, rent, internet, phone and water. I handed him the mail and asked him to pay the bills. He told me that he would take care of it that afternoon. A couple of days passed, and I followed up with him to make sure that the bills were paid. He assured me that they were, and I took him at his word.

Then one day, the power in our office was out. I checked around, and all the other businesses near us had electricity. I was perplexed and called the staff member to make sure he had paid the electric bill. He assured me that he had, but he was lying. I told him that we needed to meet immediately.

We sat down at a local coffee shop, and I asked what was going on. He told me that he had intended to pay the bills but just hadn't gotten around to it. I confronted him about lying to me, and he was defensive saying that it wasn't lying because he intended to get it done. I then explained to him the way a boss/employee relationship works. The boss tells the employee what to do, and the employee then does it. It's a pretty cut-and-dry kind of relationship.

I told him that if he did not want to do what I told him to do we would end our working relationship. We could still be friends, but he would not be an employee of the church. He responded by saying that he felt threatened. I assured him that it was not a threat but merely a statement of fact. If you do not do what your boss tells you to do, then the working relationship is over.

The same is true with Jesus. There is no such thing as partial lordship. Jesus is Lord. Every knee will bow and every tongue will confess. Stop playing games, and for the love of all that is holy... stop praying blanks.

Set your mind with proper expectations regarding prayer. Do not expect prayer to be something God never intended. God is not our little magic genie in the sky that if we rub Him just the right way, all our wildest dreams will come true. We can abandon our prayers for personal protection, prosperity and promotion so that we are free to discover God's plans for us. God does have a plan to use us. It is a good plan. It is a powerful plan. It is His plan.

But we cannot understand His plan when praying blanks. Prayer allows us to hear from God and to surrender to God. Blanks block God's will. Blanks reveal lordship issues. Blanks reveal false expectations. Blanks do nothing for us, for God or for our world. Blanks are useless.

About the only thing blanks can do is make noise. When we pray blanks, our prayers are just noisy nonsense. Our world has had enough religious noise. Our world needs people who refuse to pray blanks. Your family needs someone who will not pray blanks. Your coworkers need someone who will not pray blanks. Your neighbors and friends need someone who will not pray blanks.

Praying blanks renders us spiritually impotent. When we pray blanks, we fail to accomplish God's will. God's will is that no one would perish. God's will is that we would be His ambassadors to our lost, lonely and hurting world. Stop praying blanks, and God's power will cure your spiritual impotence and you will reproduce spiritually.

III

I Am I Do

I dentity determines action.

They say that good boy status waits for those who robotically obey the rules.

With every pat on the head and slap on the back I became just like those fools.

Bad boys do what bad boys do, because rules are made for breaking.

I always knew my good boy ways were vain attempts at faking.

– Shiloh Battles

Religion is based on the faulty notion of behavior modification. The basic premise of the rules of religion is that changing what you do will transform who you are. That is a backwards process that produces arrogance, comparison, frustration and defeat.

A relationship with Jesus, on the other hand, is based on identity. Accepting who you are in Christ determines your actions. Love is your primary concern instead of rules. Being a child of God is what drives you to act like a child of God.

Identity and action go hand in hand. Both are crucial for abundant, purposeful living. But just as you cannot have one without the other, it is also crucial that one determines and drives the other. Religion reverses the order by claiming that if you change what you do, it will change who you are. This mindset leads mostly to pretending. You can pretend to be good, but that does not make you good.

Religion is filled with posers—people pretending to be something they are not. Posing is an exhausting, futile and miserable enterprise. It is not what God desires. God never asks us to change who we are so we can be with Him, but He invites us to be new creations in Him.

Following Jesus never makes any sense unless it is done from the proper foundation. Who we are determines what we do. When we understand that we are adopted children of God, holy and dearly loved, then we are free to act accordingly. Our loving Father reminds us constantly of who we are to Him so that we are free to simply be. Being a child of God results in doing godly things.

I am a father, and I love my three children. I want them to do the right things, but I know that they struggle with identity. They are pulled in many directions to become many different things. Friends, pop-culture, teams, clubs, groups, church, teachers, coaches and societal norms pull at them and try to tell them how they should act. They hear many conflicting messages, and they are often frustrated and confused because they do not know what to listen to. I hate that for them. I do not want that for them. It is imperative to me that my children understand who they are so that identity fuels their actions.

Ensley is my youngest child. She is super-observant, bright and quick-witted. She watches her older brother and sister and learns. I tend to communicate similar things to all three children, and Ensley often has the benefit of hearing things multiple times. Ensley's responses are usually thoughtful and heart-warming.

One of the things I say regularly to my kids deals with who they are. I want to remind them often about their identity, so they are prepared to act accordingly.

I tell my oldest, "Alizah…Jesus loves you. I love you. You are my girl. You are a good girl." She usually replies with, "I know."

I tell my son, "Ace…Jesus loves you. I love you. You are my boy. You are a good boy." He usually replies with, "Thank you."

But Ensley is different. I say, "Ensley…Jesus loves you." She says, "Jesus loves you too, Daddy." I say, "Ensley…I love you." She says, "I love you too, Daddy." I say, "Ensley…you are my good girl." She says, "You are my Daddy." I say, "Ensley…you are a good girl." She says, "You are a good Daddy."

Her response tells me that she understands the relational significance of what I said to her. I think that is what God desires for us. He wants us to understand the relational significance of who He says we are in Him.

You are loved by God. He is madly, passionately, head-over-heels in love with you. No matter who you are or what you've done or what's been done to you…God loves you. This will never change.

God invites you into His family. He calls you "Son" or "Daughter." You are His and He is yours. You cannot earn God's love because He gives it freely.

Identity acceptance paves the road for appropriate action. All manner of godliness ensues when you accept that your core identity is godly. Godly people do godly things.

The grand struggle is to believe that we are who God declares that we are. It is not arrogance or vanity to accept the gift of godliness, but it is ignorance and insanity to reject it. The primary frustration that most Christians feel is rooted in this issue. We do not accept who God says we are and therefore cannot do what God commands. Defeat is imminent when our core belief is that God is a liar. Faith is gone when we believe that God is a liar.

God is not a liar.

God is truth. Do not call "evil" what He declares is "good."

If the Holy Spirit dwells inside of you, then you are a new creation. The old is gone. The new has come. Live by the Spirit. Keep in step with the Spirit. Listen to what God says about you. You are loved. You are His. You are good.

Good people do good things. You are free to do good things. God has wonderful things prepared for you to do. After all, you are God's workmanship created in Christ Jesus to do good works. That's right…you are a real piece of work!

You are a good piece of work, and you are intended for good works. God has wonderful works prepared for you to do. Your life matters. What you do and do not do produce eternal consequences. Identity acceptance is absolutely essential for abundant living in Christ.

Countless "Christians" are deceived into thinking that following Jesus is just about going to heaven when you die.

Scripture tells us to offer our bodies as living sacrifices. We are not dead sacrifices! Jesus took care of the sacrificial death business so that we can be living sacrifices for Him. That means that our lives have extreme value. We are called, set apart, chosen, prepared, equipped and released to do God's will.

When we refuse to do God's will, His will does not get done.

I hope that the gravity of that reality captivates your heart. God chooses to do His work through you because you are His. Life has ultimate value and meaning when we accept who we are and act accordingly.

Knowing who we are allows us to enjoy being in God's hands. We trust His will for our lives and are free to simply be. Our primary concerns no longer revolve around personal safety and protection because we know that God has important work for us to do. The risk involved in following Jesus is mitigated by the reality of who we are in Him. We are not afraid because we know we are His.

Late one evening, when my oldest daughter was still in grade school, I was helping her get ready for bed. She had taken a bath, put her pajamas on and said her prayers. The only thing left to do was to brush her hair before she jumped under the covers.

I was tired and wanted to get her in bed as quickly as possible, so I took the brush from her and began to gently pull it through her still damp hair. On the very first stroke the brush snagged on a tangle. I had to make a decision as to what to do next.

Would I pull the brush out and start over or simply yank the brush through the tangle? Well, because my daughter is very tough and because I was in a hurry to get her into bed, I decided to pull the brush through the tangle. I am not claiming that it was the best decision, but it was the choice I made nonetheless.

When I pulled down on the brush handle my daughter's sweet little head jerked back and she said, "Ouch," I told her to stand still and to stop being a sissy. At that point she turned around and looked me right in the eye with an evil little grin. The words that came out of her mouth struck fear into my heart. She boldly proclaimed, "I'm telling Mom!"

My daughter could sense the fear in my eyes. I didn't want her to tell mom. Not because I was ashamed of my decision as much as I really just didn't want to prolong the process. I was ready for bed, and I really didn't want to sit around for another thirty minutes discussing the proper way to brush a little girl's hair.

Before I could respond, my daughter spun around and started to run out of the room to find her mother. At that point instinct took over, and the linebacker in me rose to the surface. In one fluid movement I sprung from the bed, tackled my little girl and threw her high in the air back toward her bed. Everything moved in slow motion as I watched my sweet little angel fly through the air. I stood in proud admiration of my handiwork as she sailed breathlessly toward the bed.

Now to fully comprehend the dynamics of the situation, you need to know that my daughter's room was situated at the top of our stairway on the second floor of our home. When she ran for the door and I tackled her, she became disoriented and was not sure in what direction I had thrown her. So as she floated in the air, she did not know if she would land safely on her bed or fly over the stairs to the ground below.

When she finally did come down, she bounced off the bed and let out a loud gasp. I was concerned as to what might happen next. Would she scream for mom? Time stood still as I waited. Finally she caught her breath and began to laugh uncontrollably.

Her laugh was utterly contagious, and I fell on the floor laughing with her. After several minutes of giggling together, I finally caught my breath enough to ask her what we were laughing about.

She responded by saying: "Well,dad, when you tackled me and threw me, I didn't know if you had thrown me over the stairs or back toward my bed. So, as I flew through the air, the only thing I could think was (at this point she stands up, spreads her arms out wide and sings with all her might) 'I Believe I Can Fly.'"

I found out that night that my daughter believed in me. She knew that no matter which direction I threw her in, it would be okay. Her only concern was to enjoy the flight. This is a wonderful lesson we can all learn from.

Do we truly believe in Jesus? Do we trust Him enough to surrender completely to His will? Are we willing to allow Jesus to throw us into life, confidently believing that He knows what is best for us?

God never promised us safety. He in no way says that we will never suffer, but Jesus does guarantee that we will have an abundant life if we believe in Him. So today, whether you are thrown to safety or tossed back into the fray of life, can you confidently say, "I believe I can fly"?

God believes you can fly.

It is interesting that we are often told that we must believe in God, but we are never told that God believes in us.

God takes us and throws us into this big, wild, crazy world because He knows we can fly. Believing matters...believe me. When we believe that what God declares about us is true, we are free to fly. Life explodes with passion and purpose.

Is it safe?

Absolutely not, but it is thrilling. Jesus did not save us from death so that we could shuffle through life just hoping to survive. We are saved so that we can thrive. Thriving means running headlong into the fray. If your Christianity is rooted in personal safety, then I assure you that you are experiencing it all wrong.

When you believe in who God says you are, then you will rise up and soar on wings like eagles. God will accomplish miracles through you. Your life will matter. It will make a difference. Your world will be transformed through God's love moving unimpeded through you.

Believe in who you are so that your family, friends, neighbors and coworkers can experience God's love through you. You are God's plan for reaching your world. When you know who you are, you will know what to do.

Love deeply. Love thoughtfully. Love actively.

God will provide you with everything you need to do everything He wants you to do. It is time to fly. Get out of the nest and soar. Eternity is at stake.

MAKING BABIES

The more I gave, the more I got. I gave love and that's a lot.

Until one day they said, 'no more...you cannot love that dirty whore.'

I asked, "why not?" "He's not like us...he's one of them... he always was."

But who are we and who are they? No answer came. No one could say.

We separated and picked a side, but nobody won because losers divide.

The less I gave, the less I got. I withheld love and now I rot.

So here's the deal...Jesus died for you. I guess it's a pity that you never knew.

But, oh well, that's the way things go. Straight to Hell, because you did not know.

*We tried to warn you. We were firm and stern. We yelled
and screamed, "Turn or burn!"*

*Stubborn, stubborn, stubborn to the end. Yes, we were
stubborn. We did not share our friend.*

*Instead we shared wrath, judgment and fear. Then acted
offended when you just couldn't hear.*

*Buried beneath our angry words was a beautiful truth
that remained unheard.*

*Good news made bad by pitiful fools. A heinous work
done by the Devil's tools.*

– Shiloh Battles

2-PLY

There is no "us and them."

There is only "us."

When I moved to New Hampshire, the church I went to serve in had an "us and them" mentality. They adopted two prevailing ministry philosophies from the 1990s and were decidedly seeker sensitive and purpose driven. Both philosophies helped transform the church from a traditional New England church into something new and fresh. The church experienced growth, but over time the two philosophies morphed into a hybrid approach that created a problematic foundational thought.

The church became seeker-driven.

The seeker-driven mindset led to an "us and them" problem. The church was constantly confused about who what they were doing was for. After preaching my first few sermons, I had a string of people approach and express similar sentiments. They all basically said, "We love what you are talking about, but we are confused… is it for US or THEM?"

I responded by asking, "Who is US and who is THEM?"

People then struggled to explain what they meant. They used terms like lost and saved, churched and un-churched, Christian and non-Christian. In their minds you had to speak differently to the two groups. They could not conceive of a way to simply communicate with everyone.

I explained to them that the best way to determine if someone was a part of our target audience would be to check for a pulse. If there is a pulse, then we are talking to them. We would use the same language, the same truths, the same methodology to communicate with everyone. In essence, I explained, there is no us and them... there is only us.

God loves all people and wants all people to be with Him for eternity. Everyone was created for relationship with God. This core truth creates a shared human experience for all people in all times. We are all God's children, and God's family is not complete until all the kids come home.

Christianity is simple. We are invited into a love relationship with our Heavenly Father. His love moves through us to our neighbors, and they are invited as well. We love God. We love people. We reproduce spiritually.

Anything beyond those three things is a perversion. Much of what is commonly referred to as Christianity is perverted. It has nothing to do with following Jesus, dying to self, loving or reproducing spiritually. All of the religious nonsense distracts people from connecting to God and to His mission to save the world. When people get wrapped up in religious mumbo-jumbo, they become useless for building God's kingdom. Religion calls you to give your life for traditions, buildings, institutions and preserving a certain way of life.

That is not Jesus. Jesus invites everyone to join Him in His Father's work. The Father's work is not to build any kind of earthly kingdom that will crumble and fall. There is no more Temple because God dwells with people. There is no religious divide that separates who can climb into the Father's lap to be embraced in divine love.

Religion attempts to rebuild the Temple. It tries to restore the curtain that separated people from the Holy of Holies. Religion declares that God is for us and not for them. It builds walls to protect us from them. Religion is about congregating, circling the wagons and keeping out the undesirables.

That is not Jesus. Jesus removed the need for the Temple. His death ripped the Temple curtain. Jesus tore down the walls and told His followers to go. The church's job is to go and find and love and introduce. The Body of Christ's job is to go find all of our brothers and sisters and help them understand that they are God's kids and He wants them with Him forever.

Religion distracts the church from our mission.

The church is the most powerful force in the world. We are the Body of Christ, and we carry His mission to seek and save everyone. It is crucial that we remain true to His purpose and take captive every distracting thought. The enemy's greatest tactic is to distract the church from Christ's mission. Ultimate victory belongs to the Lord, but daily battles are often lost due to distraction. The enemy gets the church to divert attention and resources to false fronts as we fight battles that do nothing to build the eternal kingdom of heaven.

Mission distraction occurs every time we do good things without connecting them to the ultimate thing. Any good thing becomes a distraction when we make it the ultimate thing. Building a building is never the ultimate thing. Serving in a ministry is never the ultimate thing. Programming is never the ultimate thing. Bible study is never the ultimate thing. Church planting is never the ultimate thing. They are all a means to an end, and the end is reaching the world for Christ.

Mission distraction occurs when the mission is not clearly communicated, measurable and challenging. Nebulous mission statements are utterly worthless. In fact, they often have negative value. If we cannot evaluate our efforts against our mission, then we will always be distracted. There must be zero doubt about what the mission is, and it must present ongoing challenges. Numbers matter. Distracted churches stop counting. They say that it is not about the numbers. But it is always about the numbers. Our mission is to reach one person at a time until the whole world knows.

Mission distraction occurs when resource allocation does not add up to missional movement. Refusing to recognize and acknowledge failure creates an environment of distraction. When we refuse to admit that we missed the mark, we are forced to claim that we were aiming at something else. We invent hollow victories that produce no satisfaction and create a dishonest environment. We settle for less than God's best and accept awful results. Churches morph into Sunday social clubs that reinforce the worst in one another. Why would anyone give time, money and energy to a church that is not actively fulfilling the mission of Jesus?

Mission distraction occurs when leaders are hurt, offended or afraid. When the leader turns inward, it all goes bad. Leaders who are motivated by hurts, offenses or fears are ineffective at best and destructive at worst. Leaders must be self-aware and willing to honestly own emotional challenges. If not, the pressure will be too great, and the leader will be a distraction. Distracted leaders lead everyone off course. Pray for and support your leaders. Encourage them to follow hard after Jesus so that they can boldly say, "Follow me as I follow Christ."

Mission distraction occurs when we make assumptions. Never assume that people understand, accept and are devoted to the mission. Leaders must communicate the mission every time efforts are addressed. People will not connect the dots on their own. Left to our own devices, we always revert back to some version of personal kingdom building. Remember who you are and what you are here for. Never give your life to anything less than God's absolute best.

Our mission is Christ's mission...to save the world. God strategically placed you in your world to be used by Him to share His love. You are no accident. You are an on purpose. Your world is your home, your neighborhood, your community and your workplace/school. Everywhere you go is an opportunity to take ground for God's kingdom, but you must be mission-minded and focused.

The way that you view other people sets the stage for effectiveness in participating in God's mission. The most common world view for relationships is to assign value to people based on an anticipated return on your relational investment. If people do not meet your expectations then, you decide that the relationship no longer has value, and you stop investing in it. Most relationships are based on this dynamic and are tenuous at best. This world view is the primary reason why there are so many divorces, broken families, fractured business arrangements, split churches and abandoned friendships.

There is a better way.

What if we recognized value in people based on how God sees them? We would be free to love them without any expected return. There would be no disappointment and no regret. There would be no need to withdraw love. Love could reign supreme and cover over a multitude of sins.

Praying for One is a way to allow God's love to move through you to others. Simply praying every day for God to give you One person to share His love with positions us to be used in mighty ways to build God's kingdom. It is a simple prayer that produces miraculous results. When you become a conduit for God's love to move through you to others, you become alive with passion and purpose. People are no longer irritations or objects to be manipulated for your benefit. They are objects of God's love moving through you.

When you pray for One, God will give you One. He will give you someOne. God will reveal a name or names that you are responsible for. Pray for your someOnes by name and go out of your way to lovingly serve them. As you continue to ask God to give you One, you will begin to realize that it could be anyOne. AnyOne could be a One for you to share God's love with. Your senses will be heightened as you expectantly realize that anyOne could be your One. Then you understand that everyOne is someOne to share God's love with. Every appointment is divine. You know with great confidence that God has positioned you right where you are to boldly share His love with everyOne who crosses your path.

There is no us and them, because we are everyOne. EveryOne is loved by God. EveryOne is invited into His eternal family. EveryOne is commanded to share His love with One another.

Praying for One as an individual can change your life, but praying for One as a church can change your world. The church that prays together changes the world together. Churches that pray for One have no "us and them" thinking. There is an understanding that the church is not there for their personal consumption but is a tool for building God's kingdom.

I like to call it the 2-ply effect.

Take a look at your church's toilet paper. Is it 2-ply? This seemingly small detail speaks volumes about what your church values. Our church splurges on toilet paper because we care about people. Over the years, I have experienced grouchy "Christians" who were hell bent on keeping people out of heaven. They were satisfied with making the church as unattractive as possible. They loved to spiritualize their thinking by using phrases like "good stewardship" and "we don't want to be a feel-good church."

Is the alternative to a feel-good church a feel-bad church? Why would anyone want to have a feel-bad church?

The 2-ply effect is generated when we look at people only as us and not them. We want to welcome people and practice biblical hospitality by creating the best possible environment we can. Start with toilet paper and work your way through everything else.

If you splurge on the 2-ply, you are far more likely to pursue excellence everywhere else. You will have 2-ply programing, 2-ply music, 2-ply preaching and 2-ply leadership. The old days of settling for 1-ply will be over. The standard of loving with excellence is the most excellent way.

Do you use 2-ply toilet paper at home? Why? The answer is probably because you love your family and you want people who come to your home to be comfortable. We tend to give our best to our families. What if we realized that everyOne is a part of our family? God gave His best to make a way for all people to be with Him forever as a part of His family. He gave His one and only Son. God did not send the cheap stuff. He gave His absolute best.

2-ply Christians give their best too. Pursue the same excellence you do with your family with your church. Do not settle for less than God's best. Be willing to acknowledge shortcomings, mistakes and problems. Sacrifice to change what needs to be changed. Make your church the best it can possibly be so that it can be used to reach the most people in the shortest time.

By the way, simply pointing out what is wrong with your church is not good enough. You must be willing to be a part of the solution. I have known people over the years that were really good at pointing out everything that was wrong, but they had no desire to sacrifice to fix it. Find the 1-ply issues in your church, and do what it takes to change.

Churches that pray for One refuse to be 1-ply churches. Praying for One will not fix what is wrong in your church, but it will cause everyone to care enough to sacrifice for the needed changes. And there are needed changes.

For example, you may have someone in your church named Mary who, every fourth Sunday, sings a solo, but Mary is a terrible singer. (FYI…every church has a Mary.) Mary has been doing this for years and nobody has the heart to tell her that her singing is actually repulsive. So once a month, the church suffers through another brutal rendition of "It is Well with My Soul" in the name of niceness.

The church is often cruelest in the name of niceness. It is cruel to put Mary in that position. Someone should have a loving conversation with Mary that is based on truth. A 1-ply church refuses to change. They will allow Mary to continue to do more harm than good with her service while the church loses more and more confidence in its leaders. People will not bring their friends, family, neighbors and coworkers to a church service that they are going to have to apologize for. The niceness of 1-ply churches kills any chance at effectiveness.

It is wrong, and there is a better way. A 2-ply solution is to be honest with Mary. There is a place for Mary to serve effectively. Find that place. If Mary really has a heart to glorify Jesus and build His kingdom, she will flourish in the right place. What if you told Mary that you wanted to start a first impressions team for your church and that you had the perfect spot for her to serve every week? You could put her in a fluorescent vest at the entry to your parking lot and have her sing her fool head off as she directs cars into the parking lot. She could still sing, but people could roll their windows up as they drive by, thinking "Wow…this church really cares about welcoming people!"

Think about how your church does things. Do you have a 1-ply or 2-ply church? Are you a 1-ply or 2-ply Christian? It is crucial that we give our best until all of God's kids are home with His family. 2-ply churches understand that there is no us and them. There is only us.

2-ply or not 2-ply? That is the question.

A MATH PROBLEM

The enemy divides. Jesus multiplies.

The more I gave, the more I got. I gave love and that's a lot.

Until one day they said, 'no more...you cannot love that dirty whore.'

I asked, 'why not?' 'He's not like us...he's one of them... he always was.'

But who are we and who are they? No answer came. No one could say.

We separated and picked a side, but nobody won because losers divide.

The less I gave, the less I got. I withheld love and now I rot.

— Shiloh Battles

Christians are so busy taking stances that they never take ground. This is the number one tactic of the enemy. Satan wants the church to fight any battle except the right battle. The enemy wins as long as Christians continue to divert energy and resources away from the mission of Jesus.

People are taught to believe that the church's primary purpose is to be an agent of social change, a political influence and a moral compass. Nope, nope and nope. The church's primary purpose is to seek and save the lost.

Pastors need to stop writing position papers and blogging goofy, fear-laden rhetoric and get on with the real mission of leading the church into enemy territory to storm the gates of Hell and set the captives free. Christians need to get their eyes off of their "news" channel of choice and open their hearts to the movement of the Holy Spirit.

People are not saved because of well-reasoned points of view that fit into neatly labeled little packages. People are saved by hearing the gospel of Jesus and responding. How can they hear unless someone preaches to them? But almost nobody is preaching the gospel of Jesus! Churches have abandoned our core message and identity in order to fight civil wars.

We will fight about anything. We divide over subtle nuances in scripture…refusing to acknowledge that brilliant scholars filled with the fruit of the Spirit have come to varying conclusions on certain theological topics. Listen…God created a messy space for us to experience Him relationally. He doesn't want us to figure Him out. He is not a code to be cracked. He is a Father to be loved, listened to and experienced.

It takes far more intellectual integrity and spiritual maturity to unify on the core realities of our shared identity in Christ than it does to divide over petty pride-fueled differences. Cutting people off is easy. Leaving is easy. Running away from the real fight is easy.

Broad is the road that leads to destruction. It is time to look for the narrow gate.

A common argument I hear is the age-old "if you stand for nothing, you will fall for anything" line of thinking. I am not proposing that Christians stand for nothing. On the contrary, I think that is it absolutely essential that we understand exactly what we stand for. Knowing what we stand for is the only way we can make sure that we do not get suckered into fighting wrong fights.

Someone who wanted me to take a stand against people he disagreed with concerning the latest hot-button issue challenged me recently. (FYI…there is always a hot-button issue to divide over. It will seem like the most critical issue of our generation, and the fighting over it will be fierce. Then six months later nobody cares much anymore, and we are off to the next great divide.) This guy pulled out all the stops to get me support his side. He told me that it was my responsibility as a Christian leader to tell people what to think regarding social issues. He was upset that my preaching and writing did not take stands against people who believe differently. He actually accused me of being wishy-washy and standing for nothing.

So, in response, I wrote a statement about what I stand for.

I stand for Jesus and His mission to seek and save us all. I stand for people who are broken, hurting and struggling to accept who God created them to be. I stand for the church that is responsible for raining God's love on a dry and desperate land. I stand for Christ's eternal kingdom and seek His reign to be established on earth as it is in heaven. I stand not for the sake of standing, but so that I can walk with feet fitted with the readiness of the gospel of peace. I stand so that I can take faith-filled stumbles forward, marching into enemy territory, storming the gates of Hell to set the captives free. I stand so that if others fall I can help them up again, dust them off and together we can march onward tattered, bloodied and bruised. I stand so that one day my world (my home, my family, my friends, my Ones) will be restored to an eternal relationship with God. This is what I stand for.

Ultimately, I stand for grace and God's desire for all people to share in His eternal home. I refuse to waste critical resources on fights that do nothing to help more people into the kingdom of heaven. We are called to be godly stewards who invest wisely. Dividing is the most anti-Christ thing we could do.

Jesus told a parable about a master who went away and entrusted his wealth to three servants. Two of the servants went to work immediately and doubled what was entrusted to them before the master returned. Those servants were commended and entrusted with more. The third servant was afraid, and he dug a hole and hid his master's money. Out of fear and laziness, he refused to invest...he failed to multiple what was entrusted to him. When the master returned, he took back his money and threw the servant out of his kingdom.

The wicked, lazy servant in Jesus' story did not divide...he just failed to multiply. Think about that for a moment. Jesus is in the multiplication business. If we refuse to multiply, then we are not interested in His business. If we are not interested in His business, then we are not really His servants. If we are not really His servants, then we have no business in His kingdom. What is worse is that many are not just wicked and lazy, refusing to invest, they are actively sabotaging the multiplication work of the church by dividing. Yikes!

A common debate in churches surrounds the discussion about how Christian you have to be in order to become a Christian. It is an absolutely ridiculous argument, yet many well-meaning pastors and church leaders struggle greatly over this topic.

I was having lunch with a group of pastors, and one of them asked a question about prerequisites for baptism. There were about ten of us around the table, and we were divided between those who would baptize anyone professing faith in Christ and those who refused baptism to anyone they deemed unrepentant. The conversation, of course, swirled around the latest hot-button sexual expression issue of the day...Christians get really hung up on sex.

One particular pastor was struggling deeply with the issue of baptizing anyone who was unrepentant of sexual sin. Someone else in the group brought up blind spots...the idea that there are certain truths that we cannot see at the moment, but the Holy Spirit will reveal over time through our relationship with Him.

This was where it got interesting.

The pastor who was most adamant about refusing baptism to people just happened to be grossly overweight. He was eating a massive, unhealthy lunch of fried and fatty foods. As he was shoveling the food in, he actually said that he did not buy into the notion of blind spots! The irony was thick.

I remember feeling compassion for him because that is the thing about blind spots...we cannot spot them. If we refuse to acknowledge the probable existence of blind spots in our lives, we almost always become judgmental and self-righteous. This produces a certain kind of unmatched misery for Christians as an internal war wages. There is a civil war between our flesh and the Holy Spirit. The Holy Spirit whispers "grace" as the flesh screams "works."

Our internal conflict then drives external conflict. When there is no peace in our sacred core, there will be no peace in our relationships. We must make peace with God in order to bring peace to our world. Daily surrender is the only way to make peace with God. We must die to self every day. We must deny every notion of self-righteousness and humbly live by grace.

How do we know if we are living by grace? Are we graceful and gracious? People who live by grace are dripping with grace. Their thoughts, words and actions are gracious. They invite people into a relational space where individuals can wrestle with God and experience metamorphic transformation.

We must avoid the trap of behavior modification. This is a key way in which the enemy divides and prevents God's kingdom from multiplying. The church can become focused on cleaning up the outward expressions of a person while totally denying the internal workings of the Holy Spirit. This temptation is nothing new. Jesus chastised the religious leaders of His day by calling them "white-washed tombs." They looked squeaky clean on the outside, but they were dead and decaying on the inside.

The early church dealt with this issue as they wrestled with circumcision. As Paul became the Apostle to the Gentiles, questions arose regarding how Jewish someone had to become in order to follow Jesus. Paul proclaimed that true circumcision is a circumcision of the heart. His point is that transformation begins at our core and manifests outward. Physical circumcision created an unnecessary barrier for multiplication.

Can you imagine Paul's preaching to Gentiles if circumcision had been required? "Hey, guys…I have some amazingly good news for you…you can have access to the kingdom of heaven through a relationship with Jesus Christ…there's just one little catch…we are going to need to make a minor modification to your man parts."

I am assuming that would have slowed the growth of the church to the Gentile world tremendously.

So we return to the question regarding how "Christian" someone must be in order to become a Christian. It is a ridiculous question. Remember…the first step of faith is simply a turn toward home. When someone turns toward home, the Father runs. If the Father runs, we should run too. Anyone can come home in any condition…no matter where they've been or what they've done or what's been done to them.

The family of God receives wayward children with the Father's joy. We remove every obstacle that could hinder their return. Most of those obstacles reside in our hardened hearts. It is time to allow God to take out His chisel and start hammering away. Hearts of stone must be broken and revived so that they can beat in rhythm with the very heartbeat of God.

Allow God's love to come rushing in like a mighty, flowing river. Demolish every dam that blocks the flow of God's love to a dry and desperate land. The dams we build in order to divide are tools of the enemy. If we block the flow of God's love to anyone, then we are contributing to eternal damnation. Dividing is a dam problem.

The enemy divides. Jesus multiplies. We must get on with the business of multiplication. We must leverage every resource at our disposal for kingdom growth. We must expect and plan for exponential growth. We must never settle for less than God's best. We must repent for our divisive ways.

We must multiply or die.

Good News Bad

The most heinous thing the church can do is to make good news bad.

So here's the deal...Jesus died for you.
I guess it's a pity that you never knew.

But, oh well, that's the way things go.
Straight to Hell, because you did not know.

We tried to warn you. We were firm and stern.
We yelled and screamed, "Turn or burn!"

Stubborn, stubborn, stubborn to the end.
Yes, we were stubborn. We did not share our friend.

Instead we shared wrath, judgment and fear.
Then acted offended when you just couldn't hear.

Buried beneath our angry words
was a beautiful truth that remained unheard.

Good news made bad by pitiful fools.
A heinous work done by the Devil's tools.

— Shiloh Battles

Stop making Jesus unattractive! I am perplexed by why Christians so often choose to be intentionally repulsive. What is wrong with us? Our clear directive from Jesus is to go and make disciples, but instead of being attractive, we make ourselves into disciple repellent.

A relationship with God is attractive. Grace is attractive. Forgiveness is attractive. Acceptance is attractive. Hope is attractive. Love is attractive. Joy is attractive. Peace is attractive. Patience is attractive. Kindness is attractive. Goodness is attractive. Faithfulness is attractive. Gentleness is attractive. Self-control is attractive.

The church is equipped with the best news the world has ever heard. We have an easy job. What is easier than sharing good news? Good news is easy to share. You don't need to be all that creative or smart or clever. You can just blurt out good news.

"God loves you!"

"God wants you!"

"God is for you!"

Good news is really difficult to mess up, but somehow or the other we made it ugly for a lot of people. The common cultural perception of Christianity's central message is disturbing. God's beautiful truths are replaced with the Devil's lies.

"God is mad at you!"

"God rejects you!"

"God is against you!"

I was speaking with a pastor friend one day, and he seemed really down. I asked what was going on, and he confided to me that one of the leaders in his church had been critical of his preaching. I asked what the criticism was, and his response floored me. The church leader thought that his preaching was too grace-centered. I busted out laughing. Too grace-centered? I asked my friend if his church leader understood what business we were in. We are in the grace business. How could preaching about Jesus ever be too grace-centered?

I run into this line of thinking all the time. The church where I serve often gets labeled as a "feel good" church. People try to bash our church by claiming that attenders feel good while in a worship service. Hmm…how did feeling good in God's presence become a negative? Should we become a "feel bad" church? This line of thinking makes no sense.

God's grace feels good. His love feels good. Exalting God in worship feels good. Being transformed by His presence feels good.

But the goodness of God got perverted along the way.

People bought into a lie that claims the more miserable you are, the more holy you are. Now we have a plague of miserable, ugly Christianity. Christian people are often angry, fearful, resentful and bitter. They are easily offended and fight to make others as miserable as they are because misery loves company.

Churches ought to be fun and full of life. Yep…fun! Do not underestimate fun. Fun is important. If you can't have fun worshiping Jesus, then there is no room for fun anywhere. Good news is fun. Celebrating is fun. Miracles are fun. Why aren't churches fun?

Church is often the place where fun went to die.

Churches have ridiculous rules. Nothing ruins good news faster than church rules. Wear this. Don't wear that. Sit here but not there. Be still. Be quiet. No running. No yelling. No dancing. No eating or drinking.

I think that the no eating or drinking one is pretty funny. Many churches have signs reading, "No food or drinks in the sanctuary." What happens when you have communion? Why would a church care if someone wants to hold a coffee cup and eat a muffin while listening to a sermon?

Our church uses uniformed police officers each week to help with traffic control and security. We had a new officer one Sunday, and he pulled me aside to ask if it was okay for members to drink in the auditorium. I explained to him that it was totally okay, that we had a coffee shop on site and many people would be bringing drinks into the service. He said he understood that, but his question was different. He took me into the auditorium and pointed out a gentleman on the third row who was drinking a beer. I laughed and said, "We don't have a rule against it, but that's pretty weird." The officer kept an eye on the guy, and everything was fine. We did not need to have a special meeting after service to create a new policy. Signs were not up the next week prohibiting beer. We did not need to throw the guy out or make a scene.

I was a guest speaker at a church one Sunday, and I noticed one of the elders of the church speaking to a teenage boy. FYI... he was the only teenage boy in the church that day. I watched as the elder put his hand on the boy's shoulder and engaged him in conversation. The boy looked up at him expectantly, and I was thinking I was witnessing something special. Then it turned tragic. The elder took the young man's hat off his head and handed it to him. The boy's smile was replaced with embarrassment as the elder walked away with his chest puffed out, full of pride, thinking he had done his duty.

The elder walked over to me and told me what had happened. He said that he asked the young man where he got that hat. The hat had the logo of a local brewery on it. He then asked the teenager if he thought an elder of the church would wear a hat like that, and then told him to take it off in the Lord's house.

My face must have given me away because the Elder asked me if I thought he handled that wrong. I said, "You sure did, and I think I know why there is only one teenager in your whole church!"

In that elder's defense, I am sure that there was some crotchety old dude in his church growing up that knocked the hat off his head every Sunday. He learned that from someone, but that does not mean he needs to teach it to anyone else.

We have an opportunity to change things. We must recognize that we are God's ambassadors. We are the carriers of His good news. The methods we use to share it matter.

We have a saying at my church that helps us stay focused on effectively sharing good news. We remind each other in our creative meetings, "We don't do what we want, we do what works." Effectiveness at connecting people to God is our primary objective. We are not trying to uphold traditions or live on the cutting edge of creativity. We simply desire to remove as many barriers as possible to allow people to experience the presence of God.

This is true on the congregational scale, but it is also appropriate for individuals. Consider how you share the love of Jesus. Are you effective? We ought to use different methods for different people in different scenarios. Adapt your methodology to allow the attractive nature of a relationship with God to be experienced in an untarnished fashion. Avoid making Jesus ugly to people. Represent Him well by knowing and respecting the person you are sharing God's love with.

When effectiveness becomes your top priority, you will eagerly adapt your methodology. You will enter into another person's world to understand where he or she is coming from. You will listen before you speak. You will pray for wisdom as you share God's love. You will be exponentially more effective at building God's kingdom.

Suppose you are speaking to someone coming from a more scientific mindset. It would be repulsive for you to say things like, "You just have to believe; it's all about faith; God's ways are higher than yours; and only the arrogant question God." Instead you could say things like "God is the God of science; He created your mind to question and investigate; faith is not blind but is based on evidence; and we could explore your questions together." The first approach would needlessly raise defenses and prevent further discussion. The second approach lowers defenses and invites further discussion.

I sometimes wonder if the church actually desires further discussion or if we are intentionally sabotaging our attempts so that we can write people off as too lost to be found. I have encountered a strange type of angry Christianity that seems to have a sick fascination with keeping heaven small. There are churches that work hard to ensure that they never effectively reach anyone with the good news of Jesus. This is bizarre, and it grieves the heart of God.

Christians should use the most current methodology available in order to present the gospel as effectively as possible. The church is always one generation away from extinction, and if we refuse to change our methodology for communicating an unchanging message, then the end is near. Some argue that our biblical heroes did not need technology in order to be effective, but come on…if David had an electric guitar, he would have played it…if Paul had the internet, he would have used it prolifically…if Peter had audio, visual and lights, he would have set up a stage in the center of town.

Jesus is beautiful. His grace is gorgeous. His love is mesmerizing. Share Him in ways that people can connect to and for the love of God…don't make Jesus ugly!

OUT OF THE BASEMENT

Christianity is better off in the gutter than in the basement.

Don't go there. Don't do that.

Stay right here. We've got it down pat.

Antiseptic, sterilized, squeaky clean and paralyzed.

Buckle down. Hold on tight. Huddle up with all your might.

You must stay in to keep them out. Never question. Never doubt.

– Shiloh Battles

I wrote a book called "Pray for One." The premise of the book is simple. If Christians would daily ask God to give them One person to share His love with, God would create obvious opportunities for that to happen. Praying for One is a way of connecting to the heartbeat of God…to love the Lord your God, to love your neighbor as yourself and to go and make disciples.

Praying for One is purposefully praying God's expressed will into your life. Churches that pray for One experience the power of communal prayer and are united in pursuing the mission of Jesus to seek and save the lost. The church that prays together grows together.

The church that I pastor prays for One, and over a six-year period we tripled in size and baptized 2,500 people into Christ. Many find our story of praying for One encouraging and compelling, so I am sometimes invited to different places to speak on the subject. It is always an honor to share the message of Pray for One, and each time I do, I learn something new.

Churches like to take simple things and complicate them. We get so fixated on dissecting the subtle nuances of scripture that we never actually get around to living it out. God's expressed will is ignored while we dive "deeper" into study. I use quotation marks around "deeper" because we are prone to exchanging true relational depth with Jesus for the pursuit of academic nonsense.

Praying for One is a great example of this tendency within Christianity. It is a simple prayer with enormous implications, but it is often rejected because Christian leaders believe that simple is shallow and complex is deep. The truth, however, is that simple allows for maximum depth while complexity spreads everything thin. Simplicity removes excuses for non-action and prevents stagnation. Churches sit around pining over what the Lord's will is…like they don't already know!

The Lord's will is that we would pursue His mission to seek and save the lost. Period. The end. Simple. Not complicated.

Praying for One is a prayer. "God, please give me One person to share your love with." Pray that prayer, and watch what happens. Pray that prayer as a church, and exponential results are coming. God wants to release His church to reach the world. Praying for

One aligns our hearts with His and creates the proper sense of purpose and passion.

It is crazy that I wrote an entire book to describe something so simple and pure, but the book reinforces the foundational message with stories and revelations about how praying for One helps produce fully-functioning followers of Jesus. Sometimes pastors read the book, share it with church leaders then invite me in to unpack it further. The number one thing that I tell churches is not to complicate it.

But that is exactly what most churches do.

I was invited to a great church in a small mid-western town to share Pray for One. Many people within the church had read the book and the pastor had shared about praying for One during their worship services for about six months. They asked if I would come and reinforce the message. I was honored to go and spend time with some wonderful people.

I made a decision before leaving on the trip that I would go with the flow. I am usually in charge of things, so when I go to speak at another church, I like to participate in whatever they have going on and do what they ask of me. This particular church had a full agenda for the weekend I was there.

The agenda began on Friday evening with me addressing the leaders of the church. We had a twenty-minute drive from where we were staying to the church, and I had lots of questions about the community and spiritual landscape of the region, so I asked our hosts those questions as we drove. The town itself was small... about 4,000 residents. It was the type of Midwestern town where not much happens and not much changes.

As we pulled into town, I noticed some activity off the major road. Party tents were being set up, and parking areas were being marked off. I asked what that was all about, and our hosts said, "Oh…they are just setting up for the block party." I asked, "What's a block party?" They then explained that for a number of years in the past the main street of town was closed for construction for several months, and after it was reopened, everyone had a party to celebrate. The church itself was on that street, but they said, "Once you've been to one block party, you've been to them all."

We pulled into the church parking lot, and before me was a beautiful old building. It was well maintained…clean…painted… definitely cared for. There was a steeple, beautiful stained glass and immaculate pews. I took a quick look around before being ushered downstairs into the basement to begin the evening's festivities. I met with the leadership, and Pray for One was received enthusiastically. As we left town, I noticed that they were still setting up for the block party, and I asked when exactly the party would take place. I was informed that it lasted all day and into the night on Saturday.

The next morning we got up early because I was sharing at the church again over donuts and coffee. Driving into town, I commented that cars were already parking for the block party. The response I got was, "Not much goes on around here, so people will go to just about anything."

We arrived at the church and went down into the basement where I shared Pray for One with many of the same people from the night before and a few newbies. There were some good questions and dialogue, and after a couple of hours it was time to go eat lunch. Driving out of town, I commented on how many people were showing up for the block party. There were tons of young families and lots of smiling faces. The response this time was, "Just wait until they start serving beer…it'll be really packed then."

Sure enough…when we went back to the church basement for yet another presentation of Pray for One that evening, the parking areas were full, and the block party was hopping. I commented that it looked like people were having fun, and the response was a mumbled comment about it being nothing but a beer fest. On our way home, we drove past the block party again. This time I didn't say a word. I just kind of looked out the window at all those people. They were the very people we had been talking about reaching for the past two days, and there they were…all in one place. And where had we been? The church basement!

You can't expect people to be in your church on Sunday when you hang out in your basement all day Saturday. Get out of the basement and go to the block party. The church ought to sponsor the block party and provide music and free water. It is time to break our holy huddles and get into the game!

We made a massive mistake when we started calling church buildings "sanctuaries." It is funny how church people have special rules for the church building. "Don't run in church. Don't dance in church. Don't eat in church. Don't yell in church. Don't have fun in church." Most people see church as being the place where fun went to die.

Sanctuaries? What exactly do we need sanctuary from? In the United States of America, we have religious freedom. We do not need places to run to in order to hide. Instead of sanctuaries, we ought to see our church buildings as Emergency Rooms. They should be places where the spiritually sick and wounded can come for healing and restoration instead of Christian hideouts. We are worse than the Little Rascals with their "He-man Woman Hater's Club." For many, church has become "Terrified World Hater's Club."

The very place that anyone ought to know they can run into and be received with great joy has become an exclusive club where the spiritually overstuffed feast on tidbits of Bible trivia and look condescendingly down their noses at the ignorant masses. Sanctuaries for the lost became sanctuaries for the saved, but the saved do not need sanctuary. The saved need marching orders and should be sent.

So if you want to call your church building a sanctuary, fine… just make it as open and appealing as possible to those who actually need sanctuary. But remember that God's house is not a building. His house is His people. You are a temple of the Holy Spirit, and where you go, He goes. Be God's sanctuary and go where sanctuary is needed most.

Get out of the basement and into the gutter.

About the Author

Bo Chancey is the Senior Pastor of Manchester Christian Church in Manchester, New Hampshire. He is a gifted communicator who is passionate about challenging people to fall madly in love with Jesus Christ and believes that God desperately desires all people to find the freedom of living an abundant life in Him.

Bo received a degree in History and Speech Communications at Texas A&M University. He and his wife, Somer, have three children: Alizah, Aysen and Ensley. Bo enjoys sports, working creatively, spending time with his family and preaching.

For more information, visit bochancey.com.

Other Books by Bo

I'm Going to Light Myself on Fire

Pray for One

Every Day with Jesus

What's Your Problem

Another Day with Jesus

Don't Say "$#%&X" in Church!

Find these and other titles at amazon.com.